WAR AND PTSD

Stewart Bedford, Ph.D.

AmErica House
Baltimore

First printing

ISBN: 1-59129-098-8
PUBLISHED BY AMERICA HOUSE BOOK PUBLISHERS
www.publishamerica.com
Baltimore

Printed in the United States of America

DEDICATION

Dedicated to all of the people in the world who have suffered from severe trauma that has resulted in Post-Traumatic Stress Disorder—PTSD

ACKNOWLEDGMENTS

Many, many people, scholars, scientists and researchers have been extremely helpful to me in producing this work. I have tried to acknowledge all of these fine people in the bibliography. Without the help of these people I would not have been able to produce this work. A very special thanks goes to the following:

- David Grossman clarified what killing human beings meant to PTSD.

- Bill Mauldin and his artwork helped me and thousands of GI's with the stress of war. God Bless him and thanks, Bill.

- H.R. McMaster described headquarters and the lies the officials told the world about Vietnam.

- Robert Sapolsky is one of the researchers who have told us about some of the neurology of PTSD.

- The editors of the *American Psychiatric Association's Diagnostic and Statistical Manual (DSM)* were kind enough to let me include their research on the stress of war.

- A very special thanks goes to all of the war veterans with whom I have worked. They inspired me to tell the world about PTSD and the effect of trauma on the personalities and souls of human beings.

- Marjorie Bedford Donald in editing, spelling and typing. Thank you, Marjorie!

PREFACE

This is a book about stress and war. As I have been putting the book together, I have realized it is also a book about my life. I was born in 1920—two years after the end of World War I. (Back then it was called "The Great War" because we didn't know about World War II at that time.)

My father was a contractor. He and his "road gang" built roads and dams. Many of the men on the road gang were called "dirt stiffs," and most of them were World War veterans. As a small boy, I loved to ride with them on the dump wagons. These men talked to their mules and they talked to me. As a result, I learned a lot about trench warfare and "no man's land" (the territory between allied trenches and enemy trenches). I learned about the fear of going "over the top" (crawling out of the trenches and going across no man's land). I saw the scars these men had from the shrapnel of artillery fire. I learned about the grief that these men felt after seeing friends blown up or riddled with machine guns.

As I look back on my memories of these men through the screen of my psychological training, I believe I see many of the symptoms of PTSD (Post-Traumatic Stress Disorder). Many of these veterans had difficulty adjusting to society. They seemed to gravitate to road gang camps where they actually lived a life similar to army existence. The camps of road gangs were always miles from any towns so that the mule skinners and dirt stiffs had a "buffer" to society. Yes, I know now that I learned about PTSD long before PTSD was recognized by mental health people.

My Sunday school teacher was also a World War veteran. Every Sunday for at least five years I heard stories about the church and war. We sang "Onward Christian Soldiers" and we said prayers about our teachers' buddies who were killed in the war.

When I was in high school I worked in a men's clothing store that was run by four men who had been in World War trenches together. I know now that one of these men had PTSD symptoms. He had been gassed with mustard gas, and he hated authority. As I look back, I realize that these men considered their store as a type of "bunker."

I remember some veterans of World War I in the 1930s who suffered from "shell shock." They seemed to me to be pathetic fellows. They were shunned by many people and they were classified as "cowards." I know now (as a trained psychologist) that they were not cowards and that they suffered from PTSD. They seemed to have inner rage, but they were considered to have chronic fear. (Lots of people then did not understand the stress of war any more than some people of today.)

When I was in high school I wrote the following poem:

CROSSES
Beneath those crosses
Lie the bones of men
Who were somebody,
Or might have been,
Had they the chance
To prove themselves.

Beneath the crosses
out there may be,
The cure for cancer
For you and me
In a brain that's rotted
Or blown to hell.

Stewart Bedford
1938

In World War II, I was an enlisted man and I flew 49 missions as a tail gunner on a B-24 bomber flying out of Italy over Southern Europe. In addition to being a tail gunner, I was also the armorer and I was responsible for the inflight maintenance of the crews' machine guns as well as the arming of the bombs we dropped.

At the end of World War II, I finished college and went to work as the Chapter Manager of the Weld County, Colorado Red Cross. I held that position for two years while I was waiting to get into graduate school at the University of Denver. At that time (1946) the Red Cross was doing Veterans Service Work (along with: Disabled American Veterans; Veterans of Foreign Wars; and the American Legion). In the work of veterans service I counseled with World War II and World War I veterans who were attempting to deal with the Veterans Administration. Some of these veterans had psychological and emotional problems. In my forty-eight years work as a professional psychologist, I have counseled with veterans from World War II, Korea, Vietnam, and a few from the Gulf War.

In 1978 I became interested in biofeedback and started working with people in stress management. I did a thorough survey of the literature and published some books on stress management. In my recent work with Vietnam veterans, I have read many publications from the PTSD literature regarding the Vietnam War veterans. (Actually, the war was in Southeast Asia, but it has come to be known as the Vietnam War.)

In my present work, I have been doing psychological evaluations of veterans with PTSD. I also see some veterans in counseling, and I have worked with the families of some veterans with PTSD.

Post-Traumatic Stress Disorder is not restricted to just the trauma of war alone. It occurs in relation to many types of trauma. It can result from natural disasters (floods, fire, earthquakes); or, human caused trauma such as: rape, child abuse, and/or child molestation, accidents (plane, train, automobile wrecks); crime (mugging, murder, abduction, and robbery); and other types of natural and human caused trauma. In this book I have concentrated on the human caused trauma of war. I have done this partly because of my own experience with war and veterans, but also because I hope and pray that human beings on earth will do away with war and terrorism before we destroy civilization and life on earth.

I have had experience in working directly with disaster victims. I have taken the training offered by the American Red Cross and the American Psychological Association. I have worked with victims of earthquake (Los Angeles), fire and flood. (In 1947, as Chapter

Manager of Weld County, Colorado Red Cross, I managed the efforts of the Red Cross and the Salvation Army to help the victims of a flood in Greeley, Colorado.)

As noted, the information in this book can apply to any PTSD. But, war creates a special depth of PTSD since the "victims" are also perpetrators. In other words, it involves the fight and flight trauma of the stress reaction. God help us all if we don't learn to live in a world beyond war.

INTRODUCTION

Wars are costly. Wars cost lives. Wars cost money. A hidden cost of wars relates to the emotional trauma of human beings. This book is about the emotional cost to people involved in wars. Post-Traumatic Stress Disorder (PTSD) is one of the emotional costs. Here are some numbers to illustrate the cost of war. These figures relate to the Vietnam War, partly because that was the first war where PTSD was recognized and acknowledged. Other wars have resulted in people developing PTSD, but there is much more documentation for PTSD and the Vietnam War than for any other war.

- About 58,000 American service people died in Vietnam.
- More than 60,000 Vietnam veterans have committed suicide since the war.
- More than 300,000 service people were wounded in Vietnam. 75 percent are severely disabled as a result of their wounds.
- The average age of Vietnam warriors was 19. More than 66% of those killed or wounded were 21 years of age or younger.
- Since the war, more than 500,000 Vietnam veterans have been arrested. It is estimated that about 180,000 Vietnam veterans are incarcerated in the American prison system.
- The divorce rate of Vietnam veterans is estimated at 90 percent.
- More than 700,000 Vietnam veterans suffer from emotional problems.
- From a financial standpoint, I have heard that more than 140 billion dollars of taxpayer's money has been spent for the Vietnam War. And the cost continues to rise.

- In addition to United States losses, more than 230,000 South Vietnamese soldiers were killed. And, more than a million and a half Vietnamese civilians were killed.

Yes, wars are costly. I believe that the military planners would be well advised to take the cost of emotional trauma into account as they budget for weapons and war. As a nation, we have to protect ourselves, but we don't have to ignore the emotional plight of human beings caught up in wars.

PTSD is a mean, nasty, and stubborn disorder. This book is about some aspects of that disorder. The first part of the book tells about stress in general. I believe that stress is the basis of PTSD and that it is very important to understand the basic, human stress reaction as we try to understand the complexities of PTSD.

The latter part of the book outlines methods to help reduce some of the pain of PTSD. I don't know a cure for PTSD, but I have learned some ways to help people with PTSD as well as to help people who associate with PTSD sufferers. I believe that there is such a thing as "secondary PTSD," and I have devoted a chapter to that belief.

The Diagnostic and Statistical Manual of the American Psychiatric Association (DSM) outlines the criteria to be met for a diagnosis of PTSD. The criteria emphasizes intense fear and horror. It says nothing about anger and frustration regarding what I call "The Big Picture." That Picture includes the whole political arena.

Since the Vietnam War, many histories have been written. These histories include the horror of combat, but they also include the horror of the top command—the planners and orchestrators of the war. I believe that the overall or global picture of the Vietnam War plays a part in the criteria. Two Pulitzer Prize winning books describe the history of the war in much more detail than my chapter, "The Big Picture." (See Stanley Karow's book, *Vietnam: A History* (1983); and Neil Sheehan's book, *A Bright Shining Lie: John Paul Vann and America in Vietnam* (1988).)

Anger and rage play a very important role in PTSD. Anger relates to the fight part of the fight-or-flight reaction in stress. Many, many Vietnam veterans with PTSD seem to be "trapped" in their anger.

Therefore, anger and rage require a separate chapter.

One theme runs throughout this book. That theme relates to the fact that I don't know a cure for PTSD. In the discussions of treatment, I outline some ways I think that people with PTSD can learn some ways to reduce a little of the pain of the complicated web of PTSD.

One hope that I have about the book is that it could help people gain more understanding of a relatively new label for a disorder that has been around for ages. The book centers on the relation of war to PTSD, but other traumas can result in PTSD. By focusing on war, I have hoped that human beings can eventually go beyond war so that civilization can survive. I at least hope that the planners of war will understand the tremendous emotional cost of war—cost to all concerned. I don't think that any amount of planning will eliminate PTSD, but I do believe that more understanding of the disorder could be helpful.

IN THE BEGINNING

A HISTORY OF STRESS

A long time ago, Saber Tooth Tigers were alive and well. They had two front teeth that were mean tools and they ate meat. They were probably tough customers—especially when they were hungry.

Fossil bones have led scientists to believe that some of our ancestors were also alive and well when Saber Tooth Tigers were around.

We may have friendly feelings towards our ancestors, but the tigers saw them mainly as meat. I suspect that our ancestors did not like the idea of being seen mainly as meat. They were probably willing to run fast or fight hard—to keep from being mainly meat.

It would seem possible that some of our ancestors were better than others at fighting and getting away from the tigers (as well as other hungry creatures). I believe that our ancestors who were better at fighting and running passed their skills and systems on to their children and grandchildren. Some people call this the "survival of the fittest." That's the way nature works.

One of the systems that was passed on is now called the "fight-or-flight reaction." This reaction is a type of emergency system. It was undoubtedly a big help to our ancestors who did not want to be lunch for Saber Tooth Tigers. When they used their emergency reactions, they could fight harder or run faster than they could without the reaction. They probably welcomed all the help they could get when they were running from or fighting tigers. They needed their fight-or-flight reactions to survive.

How did our ancestors get help from their emergency reactions? First of all, they got electrical and chemical messages that were sent from their brains to various parts of their bodies. Some of the electrical messages were nerve signals that went from their brains to their muscles. The signals told the muscles what to do in fleeing or fighting. Some of the chemical messengers started in the part of our ancestors' brains called the hypothalamus. These messengers signaled pituitary glands, which in turn signaled adrenal glands. The adrenal glands put special hormones into the blood streams of our ancient relatives. These signals must have helped our ancestors survive—or how else would we be alive ourselves?

Here are some of the things the electrical and chemical signals started in our ancestors' bodies. Muscles were tensed so they could move faster and fight better. Hearts were speeded up to pump more blood and deliver more energy and oxygen to our muscles. Breathing was accelerated to capture more oxygen and to get rid of carbon dioxide. Digestion was slowed down or stopped. Tiny blood vessels at skin level contracted so that blood was shunted to parts of the body that were needed for fighting or fleeing—parts such as the large muscles, the heart, and the lungs. (This gave our ancestors more strength and may have resulted in less blood loss in case they were bitten or scratched by tigers.) Muscles that controlled bowels and bladders relaxed so that excess baggage could be dumped (no need to carry that stuff around for long runs or tough fights).

These are a few of the important things that happened when primitive people were in danger from stressors they faced. We don't know what the people called these systems. We can guess they were glad the systems were working. At least they were probably glad when they could outrun or outfight the cats with the two long teeth.

ANATOMY OF STRESS

WHAT IS TIGER JUICE?

The stress reaction is natural; therefore the things that happen in our bodies when we have stress are also natural. Our ancestors survived Saber Tooth Tigers because they had stress reactions that furnished them with emergency energy. I call this energy "tiger juice" to remind me of its natural purpose—to help me run from or fight tigers. That way, I can remind myself to conserve the special energy when I am upset and there aren't any tigers around.

When I use the term "tiger juice," I'm talking about two kinds of "juice"—the electrical messengers of nerve signals and the chemical messengers of our hormones. When you read the technical names of these messengers, you may also wish to call them "tiger juice." If the term helps you remember the real and natural purposes of your stress reaction, I'm glad. It could help you survive with less stress of stress. It could help you save your stress energies for real tigers.

Many scientists have studied our stress reactions and the emergency energy we all have. A great deal of careful research has been done on tiger juice—even if the scientists haven't used that term. Here is a short summary of some of the research.

Walter Cannon, a physiologist at the University of Chicago, did early research on stress (Cannon, 1932). He studied cats. Dr. Cannon described cats' reaction to danger. He listed the physiological changes in the cats when they were confronted with danger—mostly dogs. He called their reaction the fight-or-flight response. This response has apparently been around for a long time, and the human being has a response pattern that is very similar to other creatures, including cats.

Hans Selye was an endocrinologist (Selye, 1974). He was also a well-known expert on stress. Dr. Selye wrote many books on stress and he was president of the International Institute of Stress. Dr. Selye described a series of events that take place in us when we are in trouble. He called it the General Adaptation Syndrome (G.A.S.). Dr. Selye has done a great deal of research and has expanded the work done by Dr. Cannon. Dr. Selye has shown that there are three stages in our general adaptation syndromes. The first he called the alarm reaction; the second, the stage of resistance; and the third, the stage of exhaustion.

The general alarm is similar to the fight-or-flight reaction. It includes most of the physiological events described by Dr. Cannon in his work.

The stage of resistance comes after the alarm reaction stops and the creature starts adapting to the stressors it faces. In this stage, resistance goes up and the creature tries to cope with whatever is wrong.

The stage of exhaustion follows severe stress that lasts for a long time. In this stage, the symptoms of the alarm reaction come back and are usually hard to reverse. If we go into the stage of exhaustion, small stressors can bring about a stress reaction that is rapid and far in excess of the physical danger we face. In this, the stress reaction is the danger. (I believe that many people with PTSD—Post-Traumatic Stress Disorder—have gone into the stage of exhaustion that Dr. Selye described.)

The fight-or-flight alarm reaction begins in the part of the brain called the hypothalamus. This is a small part of the brain, bigger than a bean, but smaller than a prune. It's the boss of the autonomic nervous system and it triggers the adrenal glands, which in turn shoot chemicals, or hormones, into our blood streams when we are in danger. Two of these hormones are epinephrine and norepinephrine. These hormones work as messengers that tell parts of our body to do things—things that help us in emergencies. These chemicals activate our autonomic nervous systems and our autonomic systems play an important part in our stress reactions. When we run into tigers, we really do get extra "juice" when we need to fight tigers or run from them. We need our "tiger juice" when we meet tigers!

When we are in danger, our muscles tense up from messages sent by our autonomic nerves. Then, chemicals get into our blood stream and reinforce some of the things that are starting to happen. A few of the things that happen are: our blood pressure goes up; the tiny vessels at skin level constrict so that our hands and feet feel cold; digestion stops so that we feel like we have butterflies in our stomach; we get an increase in perspiration which we call "cold sweat"; and the muscles that control our bladder and bowels relax so that we feel a need to go to the toilet.

Other things that happen are: the spleen releases more red corpuscles to carry oxygen; the bone marrow starts making white corpuscles faster; and the liver is stimulated to produce more sugar. When the hypothalamus starts the reaction, it stimulates the pituitary glands. Then two more chemicals get into the act, the thyrotropic hormone (TTH) and the adrenocorticotropic hormone (ACTH). TTH stimulates the thyroid, which in turn regulates body metabolism. ACTH starts other chemicals flowing from the adrenal cortex.

All these messages, nerve and chemical, get us geared up to fight or run so that we can survive physical danger. When we have to fight or run to survive, all of these things are handy to have. We need our stress reactions to stay alive when we face physical danger.

Dr. Walter Hess (Hess, 1957), a physiologist and Nobel Prize winner, also did research on cats. He showed that stimulation of a cat's hypothalamus produced the changes that we can see in the fight-or-flight reaction. He also found that stimulation of another part of the cat's hypothalamus produced changes that seemed to be the opposite of the fight-or-flight reaction. This was a reaction that seemed to start relaxation going in cats. He called this the trophotropic response. He thought that the purpose of the response was for protection against "overstress."

Dr. Herbert Benson, author of the best-selling book, *The Relaxation Response* (Benson, 1975) did extensive research to show that human beings are as smart as cats and that we also have trophotropic responses. Dr. Benson calls ours the "relaxation response." He studied several methods of relaxation and meditation and showed that the physiological changes are about the same for the various methods. He also proved that human beings could learn to manage their stress reactions.

As you can see, there are some long, technical names in the anatomy of stress. That is why I use the term "tiger juice." It's much easier for me to remember than adrenocorticotrophic hormone—and adreno-corticotrophic hormone is just one of the juices.

EXTREME STRESS

Human beings have apparently been fighting wars for eons—probably starting when humans first appeared. In those early wars, the stress reaction may have been helpful (even if the wars weren't). Fighting with clubs, and spears, and swords takes a lot of energy. Ever since guns have come into the picture, however, the stress reaction and the special energy of stress has not been too helpful.

I speak from experience regarding stress energy and modern warfare. I sat in a cramped tail turret on a B-24 in World War II. I didn't need "extra energy" to move the hydraulic handle that controlled the turret and fired two 50 caliber machine guns! Unfortunately, the part of my brain that activated my stress reaction went right on zapping me with lots of stress energy—much more than I needed.

A long time after World War II ended, I ran into a fellow psychologist at a convention. This psychologist had done research on the physiological reactions of World War II Air Corp crews. As he talked, I recalled my own interrogations by medics after each mission. These medics wanted us to describe everything that went on in our physical systems during combat. By everything, I mean everything. In combat, we wore balloon-like bladders attached to our legs with tubes for our penises. These nosy medics wanted to know how much we put into those dumb attachments. The tubes were for our bladders—we didn't have anything for our bowels—those squirrelly medics wanted to know about that part of us too!

The following information is related to the research that was done on us.

We had an increase in cortisone excreted from our adrenal glands. That was to help protect us from instant allergy arising from the dust of battle. (I didn't have much dust in my turret due to the strong wind that blew through when I opened the door at my back).

We had an increase in thyroid hormone to speed up metabolism to help us get quicker energy from the food we ate. (That may have been helpful, as the K rations we had to eat weren't too easy to digest.)

We were supposed to have had an increase in endorphins from our hypothalami. (That is supposed to be the "feel good" hormone. I somehow missed that. I don't recall "feeling good"!)

The research showed that with this kind of stress, we had a reduction in sex hormones and a retraction of our testicles for protection of that part of our anatomy. (There were some things I refused to tell those prying medics.)

We were supposed to have had a shut down of our digestive tracts. They said that the "butterflies" we had in our stomachs was really blood being shunted away from our stomachs to give us more energy to run. (There were times when I felt like running, but there wasn't much room for that in the tail turret.)

They said we had an increase in blood sugar coming from our livers. The plus side of that was to give us more energy. However, the negative side was that the process could agitate or even activate diabetes. (If those medics could have, they would probably have made us give blood samples.)

The medics said we could have experienced "racing heart beats." They said that was to get energy and oxygen around to our muscles. (The cagy medics didn't tell us that racing hearts would increase blood pressure and could even cause heart attacks if we had eaten too much fat. Not much chance of that because lots of us lost our breakfasts when we saw the bombing area maps at pre-mission briefings.)

The Air Corp study showed that we probably had an increase in our rate of breathing. The medics said that this was to increase our intake of oxygen. The down side of that was that the medics wanted to know about "hyperventilation." (I was interested in that part of the inquiry. On our crew, I was the one that had to run "oxygen checks" to make sure everyone's oxygen mask was working.)

Those crazy medics wanted to know how much we had sweated and whether any of us had felt the hair on the back of our necks standing up. (Well, even at 30 degrees below zero, most of us "sweated out" the missions. As for the hair on the back of our necks, who could tell with all the things we had to wear to keep warm, protect us from flak, and have parachutes for last resorts.)

The last thing the medics had on their checklists related to "an increase in awareness." They said all five of our senses could have increased in sensitivity. That way, we could be more efficient in battle. (They didn't tell us that the down side of that was: hypervigilance; trouble concentrating; problems with recent memory; and painful sensitivity to light and sound.) I will admit that I was hypersensitive to both the sight and sound of "bombs bursting in air"—namely, flak.

Another thing that medics didn't tell us was that all of the above could trigger PTSD. It was not until 1980 that they put that together! War can, and does, result in extreme stress. War, in my mind, is not healthy for any living creatures.

PTSD

Post-Traumatic Stress Disorder (PTSD) is a diagnostic category in the *Diagnostic and Statistical Manual (DSM)* of the American Psychiatric Association. This has existed since 1980. In my opinion, however, the disorder has undoubtedly existed for a long, long time. Doctors during the United States Civil War described "irritable heart." In World War I there was "shell shock." In World War II and the Korean War there was "combat fatigue." In Vietnam (during the war) there was "gross stress." I believe that all of these disorders were indeed PTSD.

The Diagnostic and Statistical Manual of the American Psychiatric Association has been the "Bible" since 1952. The manual is now in its fifth revision. It is also the criteria the United States Department of Veteran's Affairs (the V.A.) uses in diagnosing PTSD in veterans. *The Diagnostic and Statistical Manual* (DSM) does not restrict PTSD to the trauma of military service. The V.A. does.

DSM I, published in 1952, had a diagnostic classification called "Gross Stress Reaction." That was the era of the Korean "War," but there isn't much in the literature about the use of this diagnostic category. During the Korean War there was an emphasis on transporting wounded service people back from combat zones to medical units located near the combat action. This was done mainly by helicopter and the practice saved many lives. The term combat fatigue, a World War II term, was still being used. I had a private interview with a psychiatrist who served as a medic in an installation similar to the one in the television show, "MASH." This doctor told me that he had treated many combat warriors who came back via helicopter suffering from combat fatigue. He said that the plan was to treat these men briefly and get them back in their units as soon as possible. He said that these men had fear of dying or being seriously injured, but that a significant number of the men had a strong fear of being seen as cowards, making errors, and letting their buddies down. This psychiatrist believed that this latter fear was actually stronger than the fear of death. He was not aware of the *DSM I* category being used during his tour of duty.

DSM II came out in 1968—at the time of the TET offensive. In this edition, "stress" was dropped and replaced by the diagnosis, "transient situational disturbance." It was noted that if this "condition" lasted more than six months, it meant that a "pre-existing personality problem was the difficulty."

At about that time, mental health workers also invented the term "compensation neurosis." They indicated that emotional problems persisted because people did not want to get over them. This term and the accompanying attitude related to World War II veterans. "When stressors stop, so do the stress symptoms." Unfortunately, I believe that some of these attitudes still exist both in the public and with some mental health workers.

In 1980 *DSM III* came out. This edition had the first criteria for diagnosing Post-Traumatic Stress Disorder (PTSD). Up until this time, "flashbacks" were considered to be schizophrenic hallucinations. Apparently, the number of Vietnam veterans with emotional problems forced the V.A. to focus on PTSD—(a new term, but not a new syndrome.) There was a carry over from previous thinking because *DSM III* indicated that "pre-existing psychopathology predisposes to the devel-opment of this disorder."

The fourth edition of the *Diagnostic and Statistical Manual—DSM III R* came out in 1987. This edition defined PTSD as when, "a person has experienced an event that is outside the range of usual human experience and that would be markedly distressing to almost anyone, e.g., serious threat to one's life or physical integrity; serious threat or harm to one's children, spouse, or other close relatives and friends; sudden destruction of one's home or community; or seeing another person who has recently been, or is being, seriously injured or killed as a result of an accident or physical violence."

DSM IV, the current "Bible," came out in 1994. This edition described PTSD in detail. The following material is as it appears in

Diagnostic and Statistical Manual IV:

309.81 Post-Traumatic Stress Disorder

A. The person has been exposed to a traumatic event in which both of the following were present:

1) the person experienced, witnessed, or was confronted with an event or events that involved actual or threatened death or serious injury, or a threat to the physical integrity of self or others;

2) the person's response involved intense fear, helplessness, or horror.

B. The traumatic event is persistently reexperienced in one (or more) of the following ways:

1) recurrent and intrusive distressing recollections of the event, including images, thoughts, or perceptions;

2) recurrent distressing dreams of the event;

3) acting or feeling as if the traumatic event were recurring (includes a sense of reliving the experience, illusions, hallucinations, and dissociative flashback episodes, including those that occur on awakening or when intoxicated).

4) intense psychological distress at exposure to internal or external cues that symbolize or resemble an aspect of the traumatic event.

5) physiological reactivity on exposure to internal or external cues that symbolize or resemble an aspect of the traumatic event.

C. Persistent avoidance of stimuli associated with the trauma and numbing of general responsiveness (not present before the trauma), as indicated by three (or more) of the following:

1) efforts to avoid thoughts, feelings, or conversations associated with the trauma;

2) efforts to avoid activities, places, or people that arouse recollections of the trauma;

3) inability to recall an important aspect of the trauma;

4) markedly diminished interest or participation in significant activities;

5) feeling of detachment or estrangement from others;

6) restricted range of affect (e.g., unable to have loving feelings);

7) sense of a foreshortened future (e.g., does not expect to have a career, marriage, children, or a normal life span).

D. Persistent symptoms of increased arousal (not present before the trauma), as indicated by two (or more) of the following:

1) difficulty falling or staying asleep;

2) irritability or outbursts of anger;

3) difficulty concentrating;

4) hypervigilance;

5) exaggerated startle response.

E. Duration of the disturbance (symptoms in Criteria B, C, and D) is more than 1 month.

F. The disturbance causes clinically significant distress or impairment in social, occupational, or other important areas of functioning.

Specify if:

Acute: if duration of symptoms is less than 3 months.

Chronic: if duration of symptoms is 3 months or more.

Specify if:

With Delayed Onset: if onset of symptoms is at least 6 months after the stressor. (*Reprinted with permission from the Diagnostic and Statistical Manual of Mental Disorders, Fourth Edition. Copyright 1994 American Psychiatric Association.*)

The literature I have studied indicates that a higher percentage of service people during World War II developed "combat fatigue" than service people in Vietnam developed "gross stress" during the war. However, a considerable number of the veterans of the Vietnam War have developed PTSD. As I noted earlier, I have worked professionally with veterans from World War II, the Korean War, the Vietnam War, and a few from the Gulf War. Many of those veterans do have (or have had) PTSD. Many of those veterans are unhappy with the emphasis placed on the "fear and horror" of war. They recall some stress during the war but they do not currently feel that fear or horror. Most of them suffer more from problems related to chronic, inner rage, than those that suffer from chronic fear. I believe that there are many reasons for this chronic rage. To understand this, I think that it is important to look at much more than the immediate stress of combat. More about that to follow.

PTSD BY THE NUMBERS

As I recall, many things in the military were done "by the numbers." (I think that meant to do things according to numbers in some crazy manual). In this chapter I am again relying on my own memories of the time I spent in the Army Air Corp. I can view these experiences now through my training as a clinical psychologist. I believe my experiences were similar to some of the experiences veterans with PTSD have had.

With me, the first "number" was the dishonesty of a recruiter. I was in college when World War II was declared by Franklin Delano Roosevelt. I was draft age and I expected to be called. A recruiter came on campus and told me that if I enlisted in the Army Air Corp reserve, I would be allowed to finish college before I was called for active duty. I signed on the dotted line. Then, two months later I was called up for active duty. (The recruiter said, "Well, you are finished with college, aren't you?)

Dishonesty of the military can be one of the "numbers" in the development of PTSD. It raises the question, "Whom can we trust?"

The next "number" done to me was the first roll call at my first formation. The sergeant called out the name, "George Bedford." I didn't answer. The sergeant called again (louder and meaner), "George S. Bedford, are you here?" I can't believe it now, but I raised my hand and said, "Sir, you may mean me. I go by my middle name, Stewart, and I would prefer that you call me Stewart Bedford."

The sergeant looked out over the formation. Then, he charged through the group and got right in my face and said, "I don't give a damn what you prefer. You are in the army now. From now on you are George S. Bedford and the S can stand for Shithouse Mouse for all I care. Do you understand me, Private George S. Bedford?"

Well, right then I began to lose some of my naive, country-boy ways. I also began to develop a whole new identity. That was something the military wanted to happen. I also took on new names to the others in formation. "Shithouse Mouse"; "Shithouse"; and "Mouse" were very common. The sergeant always emphasized the name George in roll call. No one ever called me Stew or Stewart. "George" is still a trigger for me.

I have talked to other veterans who felt a loss of identity in service. Few were as simple-minded as I was in that first formation. Many service people, however, began to feel a change of identity early on in service. Close-order drill added to development of a new and different identity. Hours and hours of close-order drill was designed to help us forget our independent identities and to respond instantly to commands. The military didn't want us to "think for ourselves." They wanted us to perform like robots. It is my opinion that this sort of philosophy resulted in lowering the sense of worth for many service people. Low self-esteem plays a part in the development of PTSD.

Bayonet drill was another "number" in the changing of identity. I believe that few recruits were natural-born killers. I was not. Therefore, the military tried to change my philosophy of life (and death). I had to spend hours charging human dummies and jabbing a bayonet into the guts of these dummies. As I did this, I had to scream, "Kill, kill, kill." Then, in orientation lectures I was told what God, according to the military, really meant by the sixth commandment. God apparently made a mistake when He (She) said, "Thou shalt not kill." The military said that God really meant to say, "Thou shalt not commit murder." I believe that this attempt by the military to change my philosophy was also meant to help change my identity and my own self-image.

Many veterans with PTSD have strong negative feelings about authority—even rage feelings. Again, from my own experience, my squadron was forced to scrub (already spanking clean) barracks floors with toothbrushes! Anyone who dared to object was asked, "Soldier, are you about to disobey a direct order?" It was an ominous thing to disobey direct orders. It was also a frustrating and an enraging thing to obey such dumb orders. The military didn't tell us they were trying to brainwash us so that we would jump at any command. I don't think that they cared that they were laying the groundwork for the rage of PTSD or the negative attitude toward authority that often accompanies PTSD.

"Inspection" also played a part in breaking down individual thinking, identity, and self-esteem. The inspecting officers always found something wrong no matter how hard we tried to be "perfect." They would get right in our faces and demand that we shout our army serial numbers, "17087825, Sir!" Another ploy to break down the human identity to a "number."

Saluting! That was another method of breaking down self-esteem and self-worth. That was especially true when the saluted officer stopped the GI (general issue), and asked, "Private, who taught you how to salute? This is the way you do it!" That type of thing also played a part in the development of conflict toward authority in some recruits.

These and many other unreasonable techniques can be building blocks for PTSD. Unfortunately, the VA (Department of Veteran Affairs) only recognizes the "fear and horror of combat." As I said, I believe that the whole, overall picture has to be taken into account to understand the "horror" of PTSD. Fortunately (for me) the things I've mentioned about my personal experiences in the military did not result in serious PTSD. These experiences did affect some of my attitudes toward unreasonable authority and toward the overall picture of war.

WHY IS PTSD SO STUBBORN?

In my practice I am often asked, "Is PTSD permanent?" My answer is, "We don't know for sure."

In my work with PTSD victims, it seems to me to be a very stubborn and tenacious disorder. With some Vietnam veterans, PTSD symptoms started soon after their time in Vietnam. With others, the symptoms can have emerged years after their time in Vietnam. (It must be noted again, that PTSD was not a disorder recognized by the VA or the Diagnostic and Statistical Manual of the American Psychiatric Association until 1980.)

I personally believe that PTSD should be considered a permanent disorder. I don't know any veterans with PTSD who have been "cured." I do know many who have learned to live with this disorder with less emotional pain and discomfort. In the following pages I will outline some of the research that could indicate that PTSD is at least a very stubborn disorder.

HANS SELYE, M.D.

Dr. Selye did monumental research about our stress reactions. In fact, he was the one who named it "The Stress Reaction." Dr. Selye was an endocrinologist who devoted most of his professional life to research on stress (an important part of PTSD). He described a series of events that take place in us when we are in trouble. He called the total reaction "The General Adaptation Syndrome." He showed that there were three stages in our general adaptation syndromes. The first stage he called the alarm reaction; the second, he called the stage of resistance; and the third, the stage of exhaustion.

(Dr. Selye did most of his research with animals—rats and cats.

However, he stated that he believed that all warm-blooded creatures, including human beings, had stress reactions that were similar.)

The general alarm reaction is actually the "fight-or-flight" reaction first described by Walter Cannon in 1932. (This part of the stress reaction was described in detail in chapter, "Anatomy of Stress...What is Tiger Juice.")

Dr. Selye did careful research on the creatures in his work when they went into the stage of exhaustion. He found that creatures in this stage became extremely sensitive to almost any pressures. When these creatures had any pressure, they "lost it" and responded with full-blown stress reactions.

Dr. Selye believed that in the stage of exhaustion, creatures used up their stress hormones. Later research has shown that this is not true. More recent research (Sapolisky, 1998) has shown that it is very rare for crucial hormones to be "used up" in this stage of the stress reaction. Sapolsky has reported that the stress response does not wear out, but that with continual activation, the stress response itself can become damaging. If a person experiences every day as an emergency, energy storage does not take place.

I believe that Dr. Selye was correct in designating a "stage of exhaustion" as a third part of the stress reaction. However, Tiger Juice does not give out, just energy stored in our bodies. At any rate the stage of exhaustion is still pertinent to the discussion of why PTSD is so stubborn and tenacious.

Does this sound familiar to some veterans with PTSD? It certainly does to me. I have worked with many veterans who "lose it" over simple things that trigger full blown fight-or-fight reactions. In these veterans I have found anxiety (flight); and a heavy emphasis on rage (fight). These veterans themselves often do not understand why they "go off," and those people around them (usually family members) have an even harder time understanding the reactions.The main point here is that Dr. Selye believed that the stage of exhaustion could be irreversible. I believe that is scary, but it is something to be considered in relation to chronic PTSD.

ROBERT M. SAPOLSKY, M.D.

Dr. Sapolsky reported how sustained stress can have numerous pathologic effects (*Science*; Vol. 273, 9 August 1996). He described research done by J. Bremner and colleagues who studied Vietnam combat veterans with PTSD. They found a significant 8% atrophy of the right hippocampus and a near significant atrophy of the left hippocampus in these Vietnam veterans with PTSD.

Dr. Sapolsky also described research done by Gurvits, Pittman and colleagues who studied Vietnam veterans with PTSD. These researchers found a significant 22% and 26% reduction in volume of the right and left hippocampi, respectively, in the war veterans with PTSD in their study.

Dr. Sapolsky stated that it was not clear whether the atrophy was associated with the trauma (war) or with succumbing to PTSD. He felt that succumbing to PTSD occurs in 5% to 20% of traumatized individuals.

Dr. Sapolsky described how the hippocampus is a structure of the brain that is vital to learning and memory. Does new problems with learning and memory (particularly recent memory) sound familiar to veterans with PTSD? They do to me. We don't know whether atrophy of the hippocampus is a permanent thing, but it adds further weight to the problems of the permanency of chronic PTSD.

DR. KONRAD LORENZ

Dr. Lorenz studied what has come to be known as "imprinting" (Lorenz, 1966). He believed that some creatures were instinctively programmed to respond to their environments in certain ways. He felt that when they responded, brain imprinting occurred. He also believed that this imprinting could then influence the creatures for the rest of their lives. One of his studies involved geese. He found that little goslings were programmed to follow the first large, moving object they saw when they came out of their eggshells. Dr. Lorenz believed that in most instances, the first large, moving object was the mother goose—a logical creature for the little goslings to follow. In his experiment, he determined to be the first large, moving object the goslings saw when they hatched. (I don't think he sat on the eggs, but he did arrange to be there when the goslings hatched.)

As Dr. Lorenz expected, the goslings did start following him when they hatched. He then studied these geese during their life times. He concluded that the little geese had imprinted him in their brains instead of the mother goose. He also discovered that these geese (imprinted with him) had trouble at later stages of development. For example, when the imprinted geese reached mating age, they ignored other geese and wanted to mate with him.

Dr. Lorenz's research has been duplicated. One scientist even went so far as to learn the mating dance of geese imprinted to him. Imagine how confused these geese were at mating time (not to mention the confusion of the scientist).

I don't know the name of the scientist, but I do remember seeing the whole thing on a nature television show.Dr. Lorenz never proved that imprinting takes place in humans, but he believed it did. He didn't know when the times of imprinting for humans occurred, but he believed it did occur. Some other scientists believe that human imprinting goes on well into adolescence and beyond, and that the imprinting has a bearing on later behavior and development.

How could this wild goose story apply to the stubbornness of PTSD? Let's consider some possibilities. First of all, the Vietnam War is some times called "the war of adolescents." We know that many Vietnam warriors were young, and (though they may not have admitted it) not fully developed from a personality standpoint. I believe in the theory of imprinting, and I believe that some warriors were imprinted by their war experiences.

A case in point, as I listen to many war veterans, it seems to me that they are processing information through a part of their brains where war memories are stored. It even seems to me that these veterans are "filtering" their perceptions and thoughts through sieves marked "war." That way, their internal thoughts, ideas, and perceptions can trigger stress reactions that seem to have no bearing on the reality of those around them. I do believe that many young people were imprinted by their war experiences, and that this imprinting left lasting memory impressions that have influenced thinking and perceiving for the rest of their lives. (I speak now from my counseling of war veterans, and from my own war experiences which I firmly believe left permanent imprints in parts of my brain.)

EXPERIMENTAL CRAZY MAKING

Pavlov was a Russian scientist who trained dogs to salivate at the sound of a bell (even though they had never eaten bells). He also did some negative "crazy making" of creatures (mostly rats and cats). In these experiments, the creatures were placed on pedestals with two holes in canvas in front of them; one hole was round, and the other hole was square. The pedestal had an air blast in it that forced the creatures to jump off their perches.

In Pavlov's study, there was a platform behind the round hole. If the creature jumped through the round hole, it landed on the platform and found food and water. If the creature jumped through the square hole when blasted with air, it fell a long way and landed in a net. We don't know the IQ's of these experimental creatures, but most of them soon learned to always jump through the round holes.

After all the creatures always jumped through the round holes, a diabolical twist was added. At that point, Pavlov started randomly switching the platform to the square hole and then back to the round hole. He continued the air blasting until the creatures "went crazy." When the creatures reached their tolerances for frustration, they literally "went crazy." They started racing around at high speeds in an aimless manner. They kept doing this until they collapsed and went into dazed and catatonic stupors. If the creatures were allowed to rest in isolation, they eventually recovered. If they were subjected to further pressures, they died.

What about human beings? How do they respond to such crazy making? We do have some answers to those questions. During the Korean (police action) War, some warriors were taken prisoner. Then Chinese officers, using Pavlov's methods, did what later became known as "brain washing." Some of these POWs survived and were studied in depth at Walter Reed Hospital. Unfortunately they were studied before the diagnosis of PTSD was developed. I suspect that many of these poor souls did develop PTSD and that some may still have the disorder.

The Korean POW's who were subjected to the brain washing methods lost confidence in their own ability to judge reality. As a result, they became distrustful of others in a way that bordered on paranoia. Their self-images were in turn altered, and I believe that the overall, political and military aspects of the Vietnam War resulted in a type of "brain washing" for many Vietnam warriors. There will be more about the political and military aspects of the Vietnam War in later chapters.

Is PTSD a permanent disorder? We still don't know for sure. Is PTSD stubborn? I believe it is, yes!

SECONDARY PTSD

In today's world as we enter the 21st century, we hear a lot about the effect that "secondary" tobacco smoke has on the health of non-smokers. I believe that something similar exists in relation to PTSD. I believe that there is such a thing as "secondary" PTSD! I think it exists even though it is not listed as an "official" diagnosis. People who live, or even associate with others who have PTSD can develop significant reactions that are very similar to PTSD. In this, I think that PTSD is "psychologically contagious."

I believe that secondary PTSD can develop in a method similar to what is sometimes called the "guitar string effect." For example, I have been told that if you place a guitar on one side of the room, and a similar guitar on the other side of the room, one guitar will respond to the other. In other words, when you pluck a string on the first guitar, vibrations will cause the same string on the other guitar to vibrate! Something similar happens with humans. When one human being goes off emotionally, other human beings can pick up the negative "vibrations," and respond by going off themselves. Therefore, I think that people who have close associations with other people who have PTSD can develop a type of secondary PTSD. In this way, people can be like guitars. (The next time you are in a room with people, and one person responds with a stress reaction, observe the other people—including yourself. Very likely, other people will also experience some stress.)

If you live with, or have a close association with someone with PTSD, are there things you can do to help prevent secondary PTSD? I believe there are some things that might be helpful. (I also think there are some things that may not be helpful.) If you are reading this book, you can be doing something very helpful. You are trying to learn more about PTSD, and that is not an easy task. Actually, this book is written for people who live and/or associate with others with

PTSD as much as it is written for those with PTSD. This is especially true for war veterans with PTSD, particularly for Vietnam War veterans.

In this chapter I will try and outline some of the things I have learned from the literature of PTSD as well as some of the things I have learned from my own experiences in working with people caught up in the complicated web of PTSD. I will try and outline some things I think are important "dos and don'ts." I will start with an important don't. Try not to say, "Forget the war. It happened a long time ago. Think about the present and the future!" Another thing that is best not to say is, "I understand how you feel." Such statements can shut down anything else you may try to do to help. And, such statements can even shut down relationships as well as discussions. Trying to learn about the whole realm of PTSD is very important. It is important to try to understand as much as you can about your veteran, but to do this it will be helpful to see the big picture—the global aspects of your veteran's war experiences and PTSD. The following areas are some practical aspects that you might want to consider to help better understand PTSD and secondary PTSD.

It is also important to keep in mind that shrieking and screaming seldom adds logic to discussions and arguments. (Such behavior goes far beyond the guitar string effect. There are times when a "time out" may need to be called.)

THE BLAME GAME

Blame is usually not helpful in dealing with PTSD. Blame, tossed back and forth can be very much like tossing the proverbial "hot potato" back and forth. When blame is tossed back and forth, negative emotions usually go up an escalator and logical thinking goes down an escalator. That way, problems seldom get solved. Also, when the hot potato (blame) is tossed, so is responsibility. When we blame others, we seldom assume realistic responsibility for what is going on. The same thing holds true when we blame ourselves. In either instance, logical thinking usually goes down the drain. If and when you realize blame (and negative emotions are escalating) call "time out" and consider some of the other methods outlined below.

COOLING OFF TIME

After either of you call "time out," take some cooling off time before you get back into a discussion. Do some deep breathing and a little large muscle exercise. The stress reaction can gradually subside with deep breathing, relaxation and/or exercise. (These are biofeedback techniques that will be described in more detail in later chapters.)

It is best if "time out" is time out—hopefully with an understanding that you will eventually return to whatever was being discussed when the time out was called.

I VERSUS YOU MESSAGES

Some of us were taught in school that we shouldn't start sentences with the word "I." There are times when it is best to consider breaking that rule. When you start statements with "You," it can be seen as an accusation.

For example, I may say, "You are wrong!" That is a type of accusation. If I start the statement with "I," I then qualify the remark with things such as, "I believe you are wrong," or, "I feel you are wrong." That tones down the accusation part. It also removes some of the listener's defensiveness. This is a subtle technique, and one that takes practice. Think about it and practice it while observing the results. It might help slow down the blame game.

ACTIVE LISTENING

Thomas Gordon (1964) developed a method for parents to talk more effectively with their children. It is an excellent technique, and it can work with other communication. The process isn't complicated, but it may take some practice. It can slow down communication, and it can prevent negative escalation.

To use active listening, one listens carefully to what another person says. Then, the listener does a type of "feedback." In this, the listener tells the speaker what they think the speaker has said. Then asks, "Do I understand you?" If the speaker agrees, then the listener can respond with his or her idea. This isn't a foolproof means of talking, but it can help eliminate some misunderstandings.

I believe active listening is something like the Navy term, "Aye, Aye." I've been told that that means, "I hear, and I understand." (I'm not sure how much leeway the listener in the Navy has in discussing the understand part.)

Active listening takes practice. Try using it when talking to children. See how it works for you before you use it in important situations.

INSTANT REPLAY

One way to practice active listening is with a tape recorder. Important! If you use a tape recorder, it is extremely important that all talkers and listeners know that the discussion is being recorded. To do this, try discussing plans to do something special together. Tape the discussion, and then listen back (instant replay). When you listen back, pay particular attention to yourself. And remember instant replay is not a "Gotcha" technique. It is a way of reviewing a different method of communication. "Gotcha" is back to the blame game. Active listening is very similar to a method used in "labor-management" negotiations. That is done with an arbitrator (referee). In this, labor may make a proposal. Before management can respond, management has to convince labor (and the arbitrator) that they understand the proposal. When that convincing is done, management can then respond to the proposal made by labor. You can probably see how this slows down discussion, but you may also detect how the method can help prevent discussions from going off on tangents.

For example, two people (named A and B) set out to decide what movie to watch. A suggests a movie. B then responds with the "I hear and I understand" part. B can then make a movie proposal. Then, each of them can discuss the positive aspects of their own choices. As a next step, each can discuss negative ideas about the other person's movie. If either A or B says something like, "You are stubborn!" the discussion escalates in a tangent. If this happens, the discussion usually shifts from movies to personalities, and "fun together" goes by the wayside.

Another thing that can throw a discussion off track is body and voice language. If shrieking enters in, movies are usually forgotten. That is where instant replay can help. Listen back to the tape and see where the discussion started to go off track. Listening back may not help you decide on a movie, but it could help you learn to use active listening.

INTIMATE ENEMIES

George Bach wrote a great book called *The Intimate Enemy: How to fight fair in love and marriage* (Bach, 1968). In this book, Dr. Bach explained a question I am often asked by wives of veterans with PTSD. "Why is my veteran sometimes mean and nasty with me, and nice to other people?" Dr. Bach believed that when we have intimate knowledge relating to someone close, that person can feel vulnerable and defensive. Vulnerable and defensive feelings can result in "mean and nasty." When you do encounter "mean and nasty," try not to shriek and toss the hot potato back. You may not be able to stop the mean and nasty, but try not to take it personally. You may cut down your own secondary PTSD.

HITTING FOULS

Dr. Bach also had some good advice about what he called "hitting below the belt." Here is an example of this (which also illustrates the intimate enemy idea). Suppose that in a period of intimate talk, your veteran shares the idea that he sometimes thinks he is crazy. (Many people with PTSD falsely think that.) You store that message away, and then you haul it out in the heat of an argument and say something like, "You said you thought you were crazy, and I agree!" That is a type of foul and is not fair fighting. Since you don't always have a referee, you may have to call time out yourself rather than escalate the problem.

These things that I have discussed are not going to "cure" PTSD or secondary PTSD. They could help you both endure some frustration without continually "losing it." I honestly believe that there is such a thing as secondary PTSD, just as I believe in the guitar string effect.

The things discussed in this chapter may or may not help a person live with or around a person with PTSD. The techniques will probably work better with mild to moderate PTSD than with severe PTSD. The techniques described will work better if all people in a relationship or family cooperate in trying to use them. If shrieking and screaming are chronic in the severe PTSD, an extended "timeout" may be indicated. The things in the chapters relating to treatment can be helpful for secondary PTSD as well as for primary PTSD.

THE BIG PICTURE

Some people, including the Department of Veteran's Affairs (the VA) place a heavy emphasis on "intense fear, helplessness, and horror" as the primary criteria for PTSD. I believe that the big picture—the global aspects of war *also* play a part in the development of PTSD, particularly in some Vietnam War veterans.

I feel that more than the horror of combat needs to be considered in trying to understand the ground work (the big picture) for the development of PTSD in Vietnam veterans. This chapter will outline some of the complicated web of PTSD and the Vietnam War. I will summarize: the political chronology of the war; the cultural revolution in the United States in the 1960s; and the rotation system and the "date of expected return from overseas (DEROS)."

The Political Chronology of the Vietnam War

The Vietnam era goes back to at least early 1930 when the Vietnamese Communist Party was formed in Hong Kong. The start of communism in Vietnam laid the groundwork for the fear in the United States of the spread of communism throughout Southeast Asia. (The so-called "domino theory" where—I guess—one communist country would knock over other countries in the way a line of standing dominos falls.)

Direct involvement by the United States began on May 8, 1950, when President Truman announced that the United States would send economic and military aid to French forces that were fighting communism in Indochina. (It is my understanding that prior to direct involvement in Indochina, Emperor Bao Dai wrote to President Truman requesting recognition of Vietnam's independence. For reasons unknown to me, that letter was never answered.)

President Truman then sent a thirty-eight-member military mission to be advisors in Vietnam. Then, on July 27, 1950, President Truman signed legislation for $15 million military aid to the French in Indochina.

In and around 1952 the McCarthy era began. Senator Joseph McCarthy started his inquisition regarding communism in the United States. His "hearings" were broadcast on national television and the whole country became aware of the dangers of being labeled as communist if there was much in the way of leanings toward the left of center in politics. McCarthy was feared, but anticommunist ideology fear spread across the land.

On October 23, 1954, President Eisenhower promised that the United States would provide aid directly to South Vietnam.

On July 8, 1959, Major Dale Buis, and Sergeant Chester Ovnand were killed by guerrillas in Bien Hoa. They were the first official United States casualties of the Vietnam War. Then, in May of 1960, President Eisenhower announced that the number of United States military advisors would be increased to 685.

On May 13, 1961, 100 United States Special Forces were sent to Vietnam and the United States Advisors began accompanying the Army of Vietnam (ARVN) units into combat.

On November 14, 1961, President Kennedy informed Saigon that he was increasing the number of United States advisors from 900 to 16,000 over a two-year period.

On August 2, 1964, North Vietnamese torpedo boats attacked United States Navy destroyer Maddox in the Gulf of Tonkin. On August 7, 1964, the Tonkin Gulf Resolution of the United States Congress authorized President Johnson to "use necessary force to deter North Vietnamese aggression."

On March 8, 1965, the first American infantry unit, the 9th Marine Brigade, with 3,500 men arrived in Danang.

In May of 1970, President Nixon said that he was not going to be the first president to preside over the defeat of the United States. He then authorized the invasion of Cambodia and Laos.

This brief (and incomplete) chronology of the Vietnam War illustrates the involvement of the United States and five United

States presidents (Presidents Truman, Eisenhower, Kennedy, Johnson, and Nixon). This is an important aspect of the Big Picture of the Vietnam War and its effect on PTSD.

An excellent review of the political chronology of the Vietnam War was written by H. R. McMaster. His book was titled *Dereliction of Duty: Lyndon Johnson, Robert McNamara, The Joint Chiefs of Staff, and the Lies That Led to Vietnam* (McMaster, 1997).

McMaster's book was based on more than five years of serious research that was allowed by the Freedom of Information Act. He had access to transcripts that had been classified until recently. With this painstaking research, McMaster's book offers an extremely important correction to the idea that the war in Vietnam was inevitable. The book is very important reading for anyone interested in the real history of the Vietnam War. I believe that it is also very important for the "big picture" of PTSD. The book also verifies the many stories I have heard from Vietnam veterans that I have counseled.

Time and again I have listened to the frustration these veterans have experienced in the futility of bloody battles for one hill or another, only to "give the damn thing back to the Vietcong." This illustrates the policy that was dictated by Lyndon Johnson and Robert McNamara to focus on "body counts." The warriors in Vietnam were aware of the futility of this prevailing so-called military strategy. They lost faith in the overall leadership and they felt betrayed by the lack of purpose for dying in Vietnam.

McMaster clearly documents the risk of dereliction of duty and he points out that the Vietnam War was lost in Washington, D.C., not in the bush of Vietnam. I firmly believe that this type of deception played as much a part in the development of PTSD as the "intense fear, helplessness, and horror" of the war. I know that the political manipulation by the powers in Washington helped create deep-seated and intense rage in some of the warriors. That rage still boils for many, many veterans of Vietnam with PTSD. I salute H. R. McMaster for documenting the real political background for the Vietnam War. Get the book and read it. It will help you understand the quagmire of the war and the web of PTSD.

THE CULTURAL REVOLUTION

In the late 1950s, the Beatniks came on the scene. In San Francisco the movement occurred in the North Beach area, particularly around the City Lights Bookstore. This "revolution" was against the so-called establishment. The first beatniks consisted of poets, artists, and musicians. The poet, Allen Ginsburg, had published the poem "Howl." The establishment said that the language made the poem pornographic. A trial was held and the establishment lost. That was an important step in the "freedom of speech" movement. And, from this came the "underground press" movement, which took the revolution against the establishment further.

The Beatniks endorsed long hair and beards for men. They moved out of San Francisco, and all was quiet until the Flower Children found the Haight-Ashbury area near Golden Gate Park in San Francisco. The Flower Children wanted to "make love, not war" and they advocated peace (and were sometimes call Peaceniks). About this time, Timothy Leary took a vacation in Mexico and discovered the magic of some mushrooms. As I remember, about that time, a chemistry student at Berkeley named Owlsly started making LSD (which was legal then). Timothy Leary then told the Flower Children to "tune in, turn on, and drop out." The Hippie movement then emerged and the revolt against the Vietnam War became serious. Draft cards, brassieres, and the American flag were burned in rallies on many American college campuses. Some Kent State University students were killed by the National Guard, and the cultural revolution turned very nasty. The division between the hawks (war advocates) and the doves (peace advocates) came out into the open in force.

By then, the draft was going full force. The war in Vietnam was fierce. Young draftees were leaving for the war and warriors were coming home. Unfortunately the draftees, and particularly the returning warriors, took the brunt of the revolution. These brave men were spit on, jeered at, and even physically attacked by war protestors. They were called "Baby Killers, Murderers and worse." Sadly, the protestors focused on the troops rather than the power in

Washington, D.C. I will state again, H. R. McMaster in his great book, *Dereliction of Duty: Lyndon Johnson, Robert McNamara, The Joint Chiefs of Staff, and the Lies That Led to Vietnam*, concluded that the Vietnam war was not lost in the bush in Vietnam or on the college campuses—it was lost in Washington, D.C. (McMaster, 1997).

It is my strong opinion that this portion of the Big Picture (the cultural revolution) played a big part in the development of PTSD in the veterans of the Vietnam War. Many veterans trashed their uniforms, their medals, and even their honorable discharge papers in disgust and frustration regarding their "unwelcome home." How sad. How utterly ludicrous. No wonder rage is so ingrained in the PTSD of many Vietnam veterans.

DEROS

The date of expected return from overseas (DEROS) was a major part of the rotation system set up by the military for Vietnam warriors. It was 12 months for the Army and 13 months for the Marines. The calendar started ticking the day the warrior arrived in Vietnam and ended 12 (or 13) months later. That way, the warriors knew when they would return home (providing they survived).

DEROS was planned on the basis of "battle fatigue" statistics from World War II. Battle fatigue was the term used in World War II for the burnout of the stress of war. The rate of battle fatigue in World War II was thought to be high. So military planners thought up the DEROS system for the Vietnam War. This system appeared to work because the percentage of mental health problems that developed during the Vietnam War was significantly less than the mental health problems that developed in the warriors of World War II during that war. However, the development of PTSD in Vietnam veterans is significantly higher than in World War II veterans.

Most of the veterans I have counseled have told a similar story, and the vast literature on the Vietnam War has confirmed the stories I have heard. The following is an outline of the scenario of DEROS and how I think it plays a part in the big picture of the development of PTSD.

New recruits for the Vietnam War were flown over to Vietnam by commercial airliners. Most of them went alone with strangers. When they arrived, they were labeled "NFG's" (in war language "new fucking guys"). They were then assigned to an outfit with seasoned warriors who did not welcome them with open arms. Most of the new guys had not been trained for the war they entered. They didn't know how to survive—and many of them did not. The more seasoned warriors were afraid that the new guys would endanger the outfits. So, the NFG's had to learn how to survive. They, like everyone else, started some kind of a calendar to keep track of their DEROS. The date of return from overseas became a type of goal. It apparently started a type of fantasy about returning to the "real world." That fantasy probably helped the warriors keep stress levels down.

When the DEROS got near, the warriors were known as "short-timers" and they were sometimes taken right out of the jungle and put on another commercial airline. Some were back in the United States in as little as 36 hours.

In the United States, the fantasies of these DEROS warriors had their bubbles broken. Their bubbles were often burst by war protestors who met these planes. They were not NFG's any longer. They were no longer short-timers. They were labeled as baby killers and treated like criminals. The "real world" they had dreamed about in Vietnam was harsh, and mean, and nasty. The nastiness even included some of the warrior's own family and friends. The "unwelcome home" experiences created wounds and scars to the very souls of many veterans. I believe that these wounds and scars played a part in the development of PTSD.

AGENT ORANGE

Many veterans of the Vietnam war who have PTSD were exposed to Agent Orange. It may be that some people know the real truth about Agent Orange and the way it affects human beings. I believe that the lies that veterans were told in Vietnam, and the lies they have been told since the war, play a part in the "big picture" of PTSD. I believe that the actual physical effects of Agent Orange could play a part in PTSD. I am positive that the lies about the use of Agent Orange do play a part in PTSD.

Agent Orange was a defoliant that was sprayed on vegetation in Vietnam in an operation labeled "Ranch Hand." It started in 1962. This operation reached its peak in 1966, but it was used throughout the war. Many Vietnam veterans have said to me that they were told that Agent Orange was an "insect spray" to help them. They were also told that it was harmless to human beings. Since the war, they have been told that Agent Orange was never used around service people from the United States. They were not told that dioxin was a part of Agent Orange and that dioxin caused cancer and birth defects.

I will state again, I believe that the lies veterans of the Vietnam War were told played a part in the big picture that caused PTSD.

These are some aspects of the "big picture" of the war in Vietnam. I believe that these factors played an important part in the development of PTSD as well as "intense fear, helplessness, and horror." I also believe that the big picture included men and women who were in the war whether they were in the bush or in the back. Participants in the war were treated the same as others. In the Vietnam War there was no such thing as the "front line." The war was everywhere, and the enemy came in all sizes, shapes, and forms. In Vietnam, very few of the enemy wore military uniforms. And all of the "enemies" were not left in Vietnam. Some were part of the "unwelcoming committee" right here in the so-called "real world."

ANGER AND PTSD

Anger is a normal potential all human beings have. It can range anywhere between slight irritation to full-blown rage. When we feel anger, we start our stress systems working—particularly our fight or flight reactions. When that happens, our bodies begin to have an increase in muscle tension and an increase in the chemicals of stress. Regardless of what has triggered our anger, we begin to get prepared for action. This process is usually in the range of physical action that gets us ready for combat to protect ourselves. If we face a wild animal that wants to eat us, the fight reaction is a good thing to be happening. If the trigger is an idea, and we are not in physical danger, the fight reaction can be a hazard itself.

When we activate the fight part of our stress reaction, several things happen (besides tense muscles in the upper part of our bodies). Our hearts start beating faster, and our blood pressure goes up. This is to get adrenaline and noradrenaline around in our bodies. The stress chemicals activate the liver to get the release of sugar stored there for energy to be used in emergencies. (I call the stress chemicals "Tiger Juice" to remind me of the purpose of stress—to fight tigers.)

When we stress ourselves with anger, we increase the rate of our breathing. Our muscles need energy (blood sugar) and oxygen. With enough tiger juice, we can shut down digestion and cause our bladders and bowels to dump (we can wet our pants and get instant diarrhea). Other things can happen, but that is enough for us to talk about here. When we activate our anger systems because of ideas rather than tigers, we can be wasting tiger juice and even endangering our lives. The chemicals of anger can cause heart attacks and strokes, just to mention two hazards. You see, the small part of our brains called the hypothalamus doesn't know the difference between tigers and ideas. That way, we can zap ourselves with tiger juice just by thinking.

PTSD

Unfortunately, anger and rage can be related to PTSD. In most of the veterans I have worked with, I have seen what I think of as a constant potential for anger, even rage. And, it usually doesn't take much to trigger anger when PTSD is involved. The following is an imaginary scenario of how I think anger gets loaded and locked in PTSD. (The scenario is not any real person, but more of a composite of many people I have seen.) It can happen in any PTSD, but I will use an example from the Vietnam War.

Imagine an average American male in his late teens or early twenties. This fellow is either drafted or volunteers for the military. He is not a born killer or a Mafia hit man, but he is trained to be a killer by the military. In fact, in training he has very likely learned many ways to kill other human beings. And, he has been thoroughly indoctrinated with the idea that he must kill to survive. This training is given to everyone whether they will carry guns or push papers. That way they all become a part of a "killing machine."

In Vietnam, our warrior learns that all of the enemies are not in uniform. In fact, he learns that the enemy can be of either sex and of almost any age. In addition, he is told by those in command that the important job is to kill as many people as possible and to count the bodies. Killing is a very aggressive thing to do, and aggression is a close cousin of anger. It can be dangerous to do all that killing, but it can also be dangerous to disobey orders.

That way, our warrior gets a double-barrel dose of anger—anger at the enemy and anger at the dumb ass orders he gets.

This entire scenario goes on in the middle of some very important personality development. These events lay down some memories that seem to get locked in an important part of his brain—apparently to remain locked there forever.

When our warrior has served his time in Vietnam, he is picked up out of the jungle one day and plunked down in the United States the next day or so. When he lands, he meets a new enemy. He is met by angry young people his own age who yell at him and spit on him. They call him a murderer and a baby killer. Of course, the military, in all its wisdom, has taken all his weapons away from him. Unfortunately it has not taken away his recently developed instincts to kill. I believe that this also helps lock in the anger potential. Our now seasoned warrior who has learned he has to kill to survive suddenly finds himself in the midst of enemies. Now, the authorities are telling him he cannot kill or he will go to jail (whereas just a day or two before the authorities had been telling him that if he refused to kill, he would go to jail). Now, our warrior is tormented with frustrations (another form of anger) and he can't trust any authority. This scenario sounds very much like PTSD to me.

Most of the Vietnam veterans I have counseled are now twenty-five to thirty years older than the imaginary fellow I just described. However, it seems to me that veterans I have talked to process information through a part of their brains that got fixated in the Vietnam War. That way, almost anything can trigger killing-rage. They know they can't kill but they can't seem to reroute the information. (This information can come from outside themselves or from within their own brain systems).

The chronic potential for anger and rage for war veterans with PTSD can come from several sources. Here are some of those sources. These sources can be at a conscious or subconscious level of awareness.

GRIEF

Unresolved grief can lead to frustration, and frustration is very often a source of irritation. In war, people can see friends blown away or killed in many ways. Some soldiers have even held buddies in their arms as the buddies died. In combat conditions there is seldom time to grieve. The heat of battle raises other priorities. Therefore, grief can be suppressed and pushed down into layers of the subconscious. Then, when PTSD emerges, anger associated with grief also emerges. Also, the emphasis on survival sometimes requires a strong macho image, and crying is not macho. Unresolved grief can, strangely enough, involve some anger, at the buddy for dying. Feelings of this type are usually buried deep.

DEPRESSION

Anger pushed down inside of ourselves can result in depressed feelings; sometimes when that happens we can get angry with ourselves. Then, we can get involved in vicious cycles. Suppressed anger leads to depression. Depression leads to more anger. When this cycle develops, anger expressed outward may seem like the only solution we have. One name for this is aggravated depression, and aggravation is certainly a form of anger.

DECEIT

Warriors (and veterans) can be deceived. They can be lied to. They can be mislead and purposely misinformed. They can be cheated. Any or all of these things can happen in war.

When they do happen in dangerous situations, these things can lead to anger and rage.

In military situations, rage about deceit usually has to be buried behind, "Yes, Sir," or "No, Sir." Stuffed anger can then emerge later with very simple misunderstandings. And when such anger and rage does emerge, it usually seems to be out of proportion to the triggering event. Veterans who have been deliberately deceived, either as warriors or veterans, frequently are very sensitive to deceit, and the usual reaction to such deceit is anger.

PHYSICAL REMINDERS

Pain can be a "reminder" that leads to anger. That is particularly true of pain associated with combat inflicted injury. The pain can be subtle such as ear ringing (tinnitus) that goes back to the noise of combat. The pain can be more severe such as the pain of shrapnel (flak) emerging through the skin. Also, the skin problems associated with Agent Orange can result in anger. (Agent Orange pain is also frequently associated with deceit so that a double dose of anger can emerge with Agent Orange pain.)

Emotional pain can also result in suppressed anger. Then, when other emotional pain is added, the emerging anger can again seem out of proportion to the immediate trigger when PTSD is involved.

EITHER/OR REASONING

Military reasoning is frequently a type of "black-or-white" reasoning where no shades of gray are allowed. Warriors who have had military, either/or reasoning drilled into them, have trouble seeing the world in anything but black-or-white reasoning. It also seems difficult for such warriors and veterans to learn about "shades of gray" reasoning. Therefore, anger frequently gets involved in arguments that require some shades of gray thinking and reasoning.

Cognitive restructuring therapy can be helpful in changing either/or reasoning. That is discussed in more detail later. I call it "rerouting thinking."

CHRONIC STRESS

PTSD is of and by itself a type of chronic stress. And remember the stress reaction is made up of both anger (fight) and fear (flight). In chronic stress, the person is frequently in a low level of the fight-or-flight reaction most of the time. Dr. Hans Selye (1976) described this type of stress as the "stage of exhaustion" in the stress cycle. Dr. Selye described how creatures (including humans) who get into this stage of exhaustion frequently respond with a full-blown stress reaction that is out of proportion to the stressors involved. Dr. Selye named our fight-or-flight reactions "stress reactions," and he also originated the word "stressor." PTSD is a form of chronic stress, and I believe it is also a form of Dr. Selye's stage of exhaustion from chronic stress. Anger is very often the reaction of people with chronic stress. It can be a combination of both anger and fear, because people with PTSD can be afraid of their own anger.

AUTHORITY

We must not forget authority as a source of anger for warriors and veterans with PTSD. Most warriors were subjected to forms of conditioned learning as the military strived to take away individual thinking and replace it with robot-like response to command. And frequently, the "commands" were issued by authority figures that did not know the first thing about survival in combat. That sort of thing led to another type of conditioned learning—hatred of all authority. Many, many veterans with PTSD have strong negative feelings toward authority. And, many of these veterans have gotten into trouble with law enforcement and work related authority (bosses). Generalized anger towards authority can be a disabling thing.

These "sources" I have just outlined are all symptoms of PTSD. Unfortunately, I have just described the symptoms. Treatment will be discussed in later chapters. However, understanding can be an important part of relieving some of the pain of anger.

RELAXATION

As I have said, I don't know any way to "cure" severe PTSD. However, there are some ways that people with PTSD can learn to live more comfortably with the disorder. PTSD is a form of stress; therefore, some of the stress management methods can be helpful. Deep muscle relaxation is one such method. Deep muscle relaxation can help, and it can also serve as a type of bridge for other ways to reduce the effects of stress in PTSD. Read this chapter and try some of the things that are outlined. To do these things, you can teach your brain and your body some useful skills. Deep muscle relaxation can be more helpful with stress and anger than with depression. However, anger is very often associated with depression.

Our brains are sometimes described as having divisions. Scientists call the upper part of our brains the cerebral cortex. Some people call it the "new brain."

The lower part is sometimes called the "old brain." I call the old brain our "alligator brain." This part of our brain includes the hypothalamus—that's the part of our brain that plays a big part in our stress reactions.

We do most of our logical thinking with our cerebral cortexes. We don't do much logical thinking with our alligator brains. In fact, when we get far enough into the stress reaction, it can seem as though our logical brains shut down and our alligator brains take over. This is particularly true when we are into the fight part of our fight-or-flight reactions. Alligators seem to me to be very aggressive creatures, and they don't seem to do much logical thinking. They don't have to with all those sharp teeth.

It does seem to me that many veterans with PTSD are quick to get into their alligator brains and to apparently shut down their logical thinking. In this way, they get into their fight modes where their bodies are preparing them for physical action. These veterans don't have as many sharp teeth as alligators, but they have been trained to kill in many ways. I suppose there are times when physical fighting is necessary for survival—there certainly were such times during the war when some important memories were planted.

When physical fighting isn't necessary for survival, our alligator brains can be more of a problem than a help. Along with the stress chemicals we start flowing when we are stressed, most of us also tense some of our muscles. (Watch someone's jaw muscles tense when they are into their alligator brains—feel your own.)

When we tense our muscles, our alligator brains read this as a stress message and call for help. That way, more stress chemicals (tiger juice) get involved. If we have to fight (or run) we need this extra energy. If we don't face real tigers, we can over react with stress—and this can happen in a very short time. We can zap ourselves with lots of very uncomfortable stress, almost instantly.

Our alligator brains don't respond to reason, but they do respond to muscle tension. Fortunately for us, they also respond to muscle relaxation. It is very hard for me (or others) to send direct messages from my upper brain (my cerebral cortex) to my lower brain (my alligator brain). I can send messages to my muscles, however. If I am stressing myself in situations where I don't need lots of extra physical energy, I can fool my old alligator brain. I can deliberately relax my muscles and let the older part of my brain read that as an "all clear" message. That way, I can fool my stress system and reduce my stress chemicals (my tiger juice). I can gain better control over my stress reaction.

Control over stress systems doesn't come about in an easy, quick fashion. It takes lots of practice. That's what relaxation training is all about; practice, practice, practice. One very important advantage for learning this skill is that you still have your stress system available when you need it. Some veterans believe that they have to remain vigilant at all times. It is hard for some of them to realize that it is possible to be vigilant and relaxed at the same time. I believe that it is. After all, some of these techniques are taught to astronauts! Now there is a job that requires vigilance and stress management.

It is hard to be tense and relaxed at the same time. It can be helpful to learn a method of tensing muscles and then relaxing them.

When you learn such a method, you will have a good tool to help you manage stress. And, since stress is a part of PTSD, people with PTSD can get some help—no cure, but some help. Here are some instructions to help you learn deep muscle relaxation.

You can follow these instructions by yourself, or you can have a friend read them to you. You could even read the instructions to a tape recorder and then listen to yourself. Either way, you can learn the technique. When you learn it, you won't have to depend on your friend or your tape. You will know the method.

First, find a comfortable place to relax. You can do it lying down on a bed or the floor. You can do it in a recliner or sitting in a chair. If you practice relaxation in different places and in different positions, it will be easier for you to transfer this training into your life in general. After you have learned to relax, you will probably want to relax in more than one way and in more than one place. If you relax sitting down, it will be easier to relax while sitting at your desk or driving your car. If you relax while lying down, it will be easier to learn to go to sleep when you want to.

Don't wear shoes or tight clothes or tight jewelry. It's best to be warm, but not too hot.

When you get yourself into a comfortable position, take a deep breath. Fill your lungs with air while you count slowly to ten. Then let the air out—all out. Concentrate on how your lungs feel when they are full of air and how they feel when they are empty.

Now think about your hands. Tense the muscles in your hands. Make fists. Think about how your hands feel when they are tense. Hold the tension while you count slowly to ten. Now relax the muscles in your hands and think about how they feel while they are relaxed. Concentrate on how your hands feel.

Now tense the muscles in your shoulders and arms. Think about how these muscles feel when they are tense. Hold this tension while you count slowly to ten. Now relax and think about how the muscles feel when they are relaxed. Get acquainted with your tense feelings. Get acquainted with your relaxed feelings. Learn how your body feels.

Now tense the muscles in your forehead. Raise your eyebrows as high as you can and think about how your face feels (think about how your face feels, not how it looks). Count slowly to ten and then relax. Now think about how these muscles feel when they are relaxed. Remember; think about the muscles when they are tense and when they are relaxed.

Now tense the muscles in your jaws. Clamp your teeth together and concentrate on how the muscles feel. Count slowly to ten and then relax. Now think about the muscles in your jaws when they are relaxed.

Take another deep breath. Hold the air in while you count slowly to ten. Think about your chest. Let the air out slowly and relax. Think about your chest when it is relaxed.

Arch your back a little and tense your back muscles. Hold the tension and think about it while you count slowly to ten. Now relax and think about the back muscles when they are relaxed.

Tighten the muscles in your stomach. Pretend that someone is going to sock you with a medicine ball and you are going to brace yourself so it doesn't hurt. Concentrate on the tight muscles. Count slowly to ten. Relax. Think about the muscles in your stomach when they are relaxed.

Tense the muscles in both legs and both feet. Hold the tension while you count slowly to ten. Think about the muscles when they are tense. Relax. Now think about the muscles when they are relaxed.

Now, try to relax all the muscles in your body. Get as comfortable as you can. Concentrate on your breathing. Think about the air coming into your body and the air going out of your body. Air coming in. Air going out. Concentrate on your breathing. Breathe deeply. Breathe slowly. Practice letting your stomach muscles pull the air in and push the air out. Concentrate on this and do this kind of breathing for about five minutes. If you start thinking about other ideas, pull your thoughts back to your breathing. Air coming in. Air going out. Air coming in. Air going out.

If you go to sleep while doing this part of the exercise, don't worry. If you stay awake, you will get more good out of the relaxation, but a little sleep doesn't hurt us now and then. If you do these exercises twice a day, you will gradually learn how to get into deep muscle relaxation. When you have learned to control relaxation in your muscles, you have learned one of the methods of managing your stress energies. You have learned a little more about the control of your emergency reaction. Remember that it is hard to be tense and relaxed at the same time.

Some of these instructions are modifications of Progressive Relaxation, a method developed by Dr. Edmund Jacobson (1962).

DEEP BREATHING

There is a short form of relaxing that can be helpful with stress. It can be done almost any time, or any place. Try one now. Take a deep breath, in through your nose. Hold it a few seconds, then, let your breath out slowly as you relax your face, your neck and your shoulders. Try to remember to do one of these little exercises every twenty to thirty minutes, or any time you start to respond to one of your triggers. This can be a help with road rage, and it's safer than cold, sweaty hands tensed on the steering wheel. Dr. Charles Stroebel (1978) calls this the "Quieting Reflex."

GRANDMA'S REMEDY

My grandmother used to tell me to "count to ten" when I felt angry. You can add that to deep breathing. Take a deep breath in through your nose, hold it a few seconds, and let the air out slowly as you relax your upper body. Then count to ten before you inhale. Try it. It can help. Dr. Maxie Maultsby (1974) calls this "Instant Sanity." He is right.

Now, read about Biofeedback and see how this can help you with relaxation.

BIOFEEDBACK

In the last chapter I said that relaxation would not cure PTSD, but that it could help you live a little more comfortably with PTSD. Biofeedback is about the same. It will not cure PTSD, but it could make your relaxation more efficient and easier.

Have you used a biofeedback instrument today? Think. Biofeedback has been around since primitive people looked at their reflections in quiet ponds or streams. When was the last time you looked in a mirror? Other biofeedback devices have also been around for a long time. How long has it been since you weighed yourself?

Biofeedback gives you information about yourself and your body—information you can use to understand or change yourself. Most biofeedback instruments are more complicated than mirrors and scales. Today's biofeedback instruments can measure the amount you sweat; your skin temperature; the amount of tension in your muscles; or the strength of brain waves in your head. When you get this type of information fed back to you, you can learn to control what your body does. You can learn to control functions in ways you may have thought impossible.

So what does all this have to do with PTSD? A lot, really. When you can raise your hand temperature, reduce your sweating, relax your muscles, and control your brain waves, you have reduced the stress chemicals in your blood stream and the tension in your system. You have learned to manage your stress energy. If you learn these things you can help reduce some of the pain of PTSD, because stress is an important part of PTSD.

Actually, you can learn to control stress without biofeedback. However, biofeedback instruments can help you learn much faster and with more accuracy. For example, it is hard to tell how much tension you have in your forehead muscles. Relax them now. Get the muscles as relaxed as you can. Do you have 10 or 50 microvolts of electricity going from your brain down your motor nerves to your muscles? A microvolt is one millionth of a volt, so either way, its not very much juice. You could, however, have enough tension to cause you trouble, even when you were as relaxed as you thought you could get. With a biofeedback instrument that measures muscle tension, you could learn to tell the difference between 10 microvolts and 50 microvolts of muscle tension. When you know that difference, you can be more sure of your relaxation methods. To do this, you would need to consult someone in the health professions who has been trained in the science of biofeedback.

BIOFEEDBACK EXPERIMENT

Would you like to try a little biofeedback experiment? Get a thermometer. A small weather thermometer will do (the kind you put in your mouth to measure body temperature won't work—most of them don't have enough range). An indoor-outdoor type thermometer will work. Color photography thermometers are great.

First, take your hand temperature. Hold the thermometer lightly between your thumb and forefinger. Wait about a minute—or until the liquid in the thermometer stops moving. Then, write down the temperature so you can remember it. Now, do the relaxation exercises in the last chapter.

After you have done the relaxation exercises, take your hand temperature again and write it down. Did it go up? If it did, you probably reduced the stress chemicals in your blood stream. You controlled your tiger juice! (If your hand temperature was close to body temperature to begin with, it probably didn't go up much—you may not have had much stress chemicals in your blood stream.) Remember, skin temperature can vary quite a bit even though your body temperature stays close to 98.6 degrees Fahrenheit, or 37.1 degrees Celsius. When you raise your hand temperature by relaxing, you are reducing the chemicals in your bloodstream that cause the smooth muscles in the tiny arterials to contract. That reduces the amount of blood flowing through the vessels at skin level so the temperature in your skin goes down. In a remote way, your thermometer can be a gauge of how much tiger juice you are pumping.

Step by step, this is the way it works. Somewhere in your mind you decide to tense or relax your muscles. You send messages from the outer part of your brain, your cerebral cortex, to your muscles, telling them what to do. These messages travel down your motor nerves in a way that is like electrical energy going down a wire. If you want to tense you muscles, you zap them with more electrical energy. If you want to relax your muscles, you reduce the amount of electrical energy. When you relax your muscles, the hypothalamus seems to read this as an all-clear signal and sends messages to reduce the stress hormones—tiger juice—in your bloodstream. When the stress chemicals are reduced, the smooth muscles in your arterials allow the vessels to enlarge. When the vessels enlarge, you have more blood flowing through them and your skin temperature goes up. In this way, you can decide to raise or lower your hand temperature. You can decide to control your stress energy. Remember, though, it will take a lot of practice before you are able to do this quickly.

If you are having a lot of stress, your hand temperature could be less than 70 degrees Fahrenheit, or 20 degrees Celsius. If you don't have much stress chemical in your bloodstream, your hand temperature will be just a little below body temperature.

After you have practiced relaxation and have recorded your hand temperature a number of times, you will get good at guessing. You will have incorporated a biofeedback method into your own system.

Try another experiment. Take your thermometer with you wherever you go. When you think you are experiencing some stress, take your hand temperature. If your hand temperature is low, try to relax. See if you can raise your hand temperature right on the spot. (If you are having stress because you are running from a tiger, forget it. Nature knows best when it comes to real tigers.)

If you are experiencing rage, which is a frequent part of PTSD, your hand temperature may or may not drop. Some people experience some blood vessel changes that are different for rage than for other stress. However, using the relaxation and biofeedback methods can also help with the physiological results of rage if you practice long enough.

Keep in mind that hand temperature is just one of the things you can change when you are into your stress reaction (when your blood runs hot or cold). In your fight-or-flight reaction, your rectal and bladder sphincters can try to open (when you have the you-know-what scared out of you, or you are pissed off.) Your digestion can be interrupted (you have butterflies in your stomach). You can sweat a lot (waking up with cold sweats can be an example). Even your hair can react (you can bristle with anger).

When you change your hand temperature, you are probably changing other things in your body. These are things you need to have happen when you deal with tigers—things you do not need to have happen when you deal with bosses, employees, teachers, students, parents, kids, doctors, patients, relatives and the VA. You do need some of your stress energy to deal with these non-tigers, but it is important to learn to manage your stress reaction so that you don't waste stress energy and end up with stress of stress. Your biofeedback systems can help you in this respect.

In the next chapter we will talk about how you can use "Instant Replay" along with relaxation and biofeedback. That could help you reroute some of your thoughts that automatically go through your PTSD memories when you encounter your "triggers." Bill Mauldin had an excellent cartoon about triggers in his book *Up Front* (Mauldin, 1945).

Triggers that come from war may represent memories that are decades old. However, those memories seem to get routed through war memories and bring about some of the same kind of reaction that occurred when the trigger memories were laid down.

INSTANT REPLAY

Most people know about instant replay on television. Sometimes we see an event, a sports play, or an accident over and over and over.

In the fast-paced electronic age in which we live, instant replays can be helpful to understand things that have happened. That can be true on television, and it can be true in our everyday lives. It can even be a way to help manage stress. This chapter will describe how the method of instant replay can be combined with the relaxation and biofeedback methods we have just covered. It comes from my book, *Instant Replay*, published by the Institute of Rational Living (Bedford, 1974).

To use this method, start keeping track of what I call "rough spots." A rough spot can be almost any event or experience that was unpleasant or stressful. Common rough spots associated with PTSD usually relate to either anger or fear. These emotions relate to fight-or-flight reactions. At first, you might want to make a few notes about your rough spots. When you are describing your rough spots, be sure to include what the trigger was; what emotion you experienced; and what your reaction included. Your reaction may have been either words or actions.

A word of caution. Flashbacks can be instant replays. While you are learning to use this technique, practice on less threatening events. Here are some examples of rough spots. (These are examples only, and not related to real people or actual events.)

X was driving on a busy street. Another driver cut in front of him and forced X to put on the brakes to avoid an accident. X reacted with rage (road rage) and hit the car horn with his right hand while flipping off the other driver with his left hand. The other driver just pulled away, laughing. X was caught in traffic and could do little else but honk, yell, and beat his fist on the steering wheel. Unfortunately, his rage lasted for some time.

Y tripped on a child's toy that was left in the middle of the room. Y reacted with immediate rage and smashed the toy. His rage also lasted for some time and involved fuming, and yelling for all to hear, including the neighbors.

Z had to write a check in a store and felt panic when he couldn't remember the date. His hands began to shake and he started sweating. He felt like running out of the store, but he froze and had his wife finish the check.

All three of these reactions could be rough spots for almost anyone. However, for someone with PTSD, the duration of this reaction can be an important factor. Rage and panic that last for more than a minute or two can be painful. And, what the people think to themselves about their reactions can also be an important factor. That part can also be included in the procedure of instant replay.

To follow the use of instant replay in stress management, the person who has had the rough spot does the relaxation and biofeedback exercise. Then, when they are relaxed, they try to remember how they felt during and after the whole thing that happened. Here, it is important to consider physical, as well as emotional feelings. (This is because some people with PTSD are not always aware of the feelings they have, particularly while they are having them.)

If thinking about the feelings while relaxing starts the feelings again, the person can refocus on relaxation.

After focusing on (and identifying) feelings, the person doing the instant replay could try and remember what action took place. Here, it is important for the person to clearly associate feelings and actions. (Actions can be either verbal or physical.) Again, it is important for the person to stay as relaxed as possible while doing instant replays, because relaxed muscles slow down stress chemicals (tiger juice).

The next part of the procedure involves thinking and rethinking thoughts and ideas that people have had about the initial event. The idea here is that the event and what the people thought to themselves about the event resulted in the stress reaction. This may sound revolutionary, but it really comes from ancient philosophy. Epicetus, a philosopher who lived before Christ, said, "People are not upset by things, but by what they think to themselves about things." And, keep in mind that Epicetus was a slave when he came up with that idea.

Doing this kind of thinking does not involve the deep level subconscious. It does involve thoughts that people can have of which they are unaware. Let's look at our hypothetical people, X, Y, and Z, when they tried instant replay.

After much practice (and some reluctance), all three learned to relax, use biofeedback, and raise their hand temperatures.

After his road rage, X relaxed and did an instant replay of the event. He was not surprised when he identified his emotion as anger feelings. He was surprised when he began to remember the physical feelings. He identified a racing heart; tense jaw muscles and gritting teeth; tight fists (except for one finger); rapid and shallow breathing; an urge to urinate (he was pissed off); leg trembling; and, a flushed face. He also remembered that these feelings lasted for a long time.

X had some trouble with the thinking part. He said, "I just automatically get pissed when someone cuts me off in traffic. I don't think. I just react!"

When he thought further, he came up with things he told the other driver, but he still had trouble remembering what he thought to himself. After several instant replay reruns, he began to remember thinking to himself that the other driver had taken his "right-of-way." Then he remembered other times that people had ignored his "rights." That led to ideas X had about authority and other situations where he had very little control. After doing instant replays on similar triggers for rage, he began asking himself, "Are these things really life threatening?"

Ideas of that type brought X to the realization that extreme stress is really more life threatening than most of the triggers he had. And that is the key message that can be understood through relaxation, biofeedback and instant replay.

Y came to some of the same conclusions. Both X and Y came to realize that stress to most of their triggers to rage were dangerous to their health and actual lives.

Z followed the same procedures and came to realize that the

emotion he felt was fear and anxiety. He remembered that he usually felt that way while writing checks—or writing almost anything in public. In his replays, he remembered that he often wondered what other people thought of him when his hands shook while writing. He finally, after many reruns, came to realize that his body was seldom in danger in relation to what people thought of him. He decided that his self-image was in danger, not his body or life. Realizing this didn't change his hand shaking, but it did change what he thought to himself when he was in public.

All three of our imaginary people suffered from PTSD. All three were war veterans. All three reacted to their triggers by running the experiences through their war memories. That is typical of people with PTSD. Their relaxation, biofeedback and instant replay exercises didn't change their "instant reactions." It did change their recovery times. By realizing some of the thoughts they had they learned to "reroute" some of the ideas that they had about stress. When they learned to reroute their thinking, they cut down on their "stress of stress." That in turn helped them to be a little more comfortable with their PTSD, and that is one of the main purposes of this book.

FLASHBACKS

Flashbacks are special kinds of instant replays. They are common to people with PTSD. In flashbacks, people with PTSD re-experience something associated with the original traumatic event (or events). The people with whom I have worked that have experienced flashbacks have told me about their flashbacks. One veteran described what he called "three dimensions of flashbacks." The first dimension involved having a memory "flash in his mind." The second dimension involved a memory plus a strong emotional reaction that momentarily disoriented him. The third dimension of flashback involved a perception that he was actually back in the war zone.

It should be noted here that flashbacks are not restricted to war PTSD. When I was working with the Red Cross, counseling earthquake victims after the Los Angeles earthquake, many of them experienced flashbacks of all three dimensions. I witnessed many of these as they occurred.

Flashbacks can be triggered by experiences, or they can occur spontaneously, "out of the blue," so to speak. They can be of short duration, or they can last for several hours. The ones that usually last the longest are the third dimension flashback. These can be very traumatic, and even dangerous, if the person having the flashback has a weapon handy. I suspect that there are veterans in prison who have "gone off" with flashbacks and weapons. I also know of instances where law enforcement SWAT teams have killed veterans during these types of flashback.

Now, back to instant replays. I said earlier that people should not attempt the instant replay method with flashbacks. That is particularly true for three-dimensional flashbacks. However, it is possible to use relaxation and biofeedback after a flashback to help reduce the stress chemicals (tiger juice) that were activated by the flashback. Those methods can reduce the time spent in stress (and even shock) after the flashbacks. Instant replay can be used for the first dimension type flashback. That method can help identify subconscious "triggers" that set off flashbacks. It can also help the person learn some of the things they think to themselves about the fact that they have flashbacks. That can be very important, because some people lose confidence in themselves. Or, some people can even think they are "losing their minds."

I don't know all of the neurological aspects of three-dimensional flashbacks. I have never had a three dimensional flashback. I have witnessed a few. It is almost as though a part of the brain of the person is dreaming while the person is still awake. The official name is a "dissociative reaction," which can be a symptom of severe PTSD.

I believe that there is a type of conditioned learning involved in most flashbacks. Pavlov's dog learned by conditioning methods. Pavlov fed his dog a food pellet every time he (Pavlov) rang a bell. Then, the dog expected food whenever Pavlov rang a bell. That (the food) is called positive reenforcement. Pavlov also did some negative work with dogs and other animals, but we don't hear as much about that work as we do the bell, the food, and the salivating. Most PTSD flashbacks are from negative conditioning.

Bill Mauldon's cartoon of Willie and Joe represents negative conditioning associated with a sound. Joe is zipping a zipper and Willie is hitting the ground, obviously associating the sound with danger. We could carry that example further and speculate that Willie could have flashbacks of the dangers of war (zipping bullets) whenever he heard other zippers after the war. That is how flashbacks work.

Some triggers for flashbacks can gradually become extinguished, some can remain for years, or forever for a person with PTSD. In these people, trauma has occurred in relation to some sensation (sound, smell, sight, feeling, or even taste). Then, when the person that has been conditioned reexperiences the sensation, they react in the way they have learned. For example, Willie probably learned to fall down flat when he heard bullets "zipping." That way, he learned to survive in war. If he had flashbacks, he responded to zippers rather than zipping bullets.

Flashbacks can be embarrassing. For example, let's assume that zippers caused flashbacks for Willie. His conditioned response was to drop flat on the ground when he heard a zipper being zipped. It is quite possible that Willie could be in situations where he was the only one to drop to the ground when a zipper was zipped. Other people, who did not associate zippers with bullets, would not understand Willie. They might even laugh and think that Willie was crazy. If Willie did have PTSD, people would not understand that, either.

I would like to give some more examples of flashbacks, but I don't have permission to reveal the things I have heard. So, I guess I will describe some of my own flashbacks, and mine were learned more than fifty years ago. I have never had a three dimensional flashback, but I still have some of the first two.

My house is in a flight pattern for the local airport. Sometimes when a four engine plane comes in for a landing, I reexperience the fear I felt when a B-24 Bomber pilot mistook the lights in our row of tents for the runway lights. Fortunately for us (those in the tents), the pilot pulled up in time to miss our tents, but the B-24 ended up "cartwheeling" on the airfield in a ball of flames. In my flashbacks, I have the urge to "seek cover" when I hear a big plane landing, even though in my rational mind, I know I am safe.

Another flashback happened when my children were little. I was driving in the country where crop dusting planes were flying low over fields. I saw one coming in fast. Without thinking, I maneuvered the car for the best angle to shoot it down. The adult passengers were petrified (and angry). The kids loved it. Fortunately, my machine guns malfunctioned so we didn't have to paint a crop duster plane on the hood of the car.

One of my most troubling flashbacks occurs whenever I see reruns of the Oklahoma bombing of the federal building. Whenever I see the building and the trauma of the victims, I flashback on bomb runs where our bombs missed military targets and exploded in civilian areas—with bombs that I, as armorer, had personally armed. I have never actually thought I was back in the bomb bay setting the bombs to explode (third dimension). But I have come close.

I had another flashback while I was teaching a college class in stress management. Someone in the class asked me what sort of stressful experiences I had had. I immediately described crawling into the bomb bay; arming bombs, and then seeing the bombs miss military targets and hit civilian areas. As I talked, I noticed the color draining out of an older woman's face. She looked like she was going to faint, so I asked her what was wrong. She said, in a broken Austrian accent, "I was on the ground in Vienna when those bombs hit." In that flashback, I felt color draining from my face and I thought I was going to faint. (Our crew had bombed Vienna several times.)

On a positive footnote, the Austrian woman and I were both able to use relaxation, deep breathing, and biofeedback for our flashback instant replays in the class.

As I noted, the triggers for most of my flashbacks were laid down more than fifty years ago. Some people still tell me to "just forget the war. It's over." That is much easier said than done. Plus, that statement can be a trigger for an emotion other than fear and horror. Fortunately, I've never locked and loaded my machine guns when someone has told me that, but I have come close.

One thing to remember in relation to PTSD flashbacks, is that relaxation, biofeedback, and instant replay probably won't eliminate the flashbacks. However, those things can help reduce the stress aftermath of the flashbacks. Those methods are worthwhile stress management techniques, even though they won't cure PTSD.

As I "flashback" on my nearly fifty years of being a professional psychologist, I have never come up with a cure for PTSD. I have learned some ways to be more comfortable with PTSD, including my own. Trying to learn about the complicated web of PTSD has helped. Learning that it is difficult to be tense and relaxed at the same time has also helped. Relaxing and breathing easy have helped. Doing instant replays and rerouting my thinking has also helped. Support groups have helped. And, talking to other victims of PTSD has also helped. Medication can help, but none of these things will likely "cure" PTSD.

TREATMENT

Treatment for PTSD can vary all the way from simple self-help methods, to professional help, to inpatient treatment by the Department of Veteran's Affairs—the VA. In this chapter we will discuss treatment and summarize the range of options. I will not be discussing inpatient treatment. The VA maintains many inpatient facilities for the treatment of PTSD. If such treatment is needed, you must contact the VA.

SELF-HELP

This book itself has some elements of self-help. It offers one important part of self-help—information. It is very important to understand PTSD. PTSD is not a new disorder, but it has not been recognized as a disorder for very long. As a result, many people do not know about it, or understand it. This is in spite of the fact that hundreds of books have been written about the wars and traumas that cause PTSD.

An exercise in self-help can be a self-inventory. This follows along the lines of Reinhold Niebuhr's famous prayer: "God grant me the serenity to accept the things I cannot change, the courage to change the things I can, and the wisdom to know the difference." Reverend Niebuhr wrote those words in 1934. The prayer has been used in many ways, including Alcoholics Anonymous. It certainly can apply to PTSD.

In this self-help procedure, you fold a piece of paper in two (lengthwise). On one side of the paper put a plus, and on the other side a minus. Then, list the things you like about yourself on the plus side. On the minus side, list the things about yourself you don't like.

You may not want to change anything on the plus side (unless you consult with others). You may want to change some of the things on the minus side. Underline the things you cannot change. Put a check mark by the ones you can, and want to change. Then, relax, do a biofeedback exercise and an instant replay. Try to find out what you think to yourself about making the changes that you can. Try to figure out why you haven't made the changes. You can talk this over with a close, significant other for feedback. That could give you a reality check.

As a second step, use the procedures to find out what you think of yourself about the things you cannot change. The thoughts you have about the things you cannot change may be causing you stress. Use the re-routing techniques to reduce whatever self-blame thoughts you have that may be causing depression and rage; with those emotions, you are probably wasting tiger juice.

Both of these procedures can give you a check on your self-image. And, remember it is your self-image that may be in danger instead of your body when the tiger juice starts to flow.

Read self-help books, but always have a grain or two of salt handy when you do. That applies to this book as well as any book. Learn to trust your own judgment. If you do nothing else, self-help procedures can be worthwhile.

SUPPORT GROUPS

Talking to other people who have PTSD (or are exposed to it) can be helpful. Sharing experiences can help with a feeling of isolation. A very common remark for an NFG (New Fucking Guy—in army language) is, "I had no idea anyone else felt this way." That can be very therapeutic. Actually, a support group for PTSD is made up of "experts" in PTSD.

Support groups don't have to focus entirely on war experiences. One helpful thing is learning how other people with PTSD cope with the disorder. It can be helpful to focus on the experiences that caused PTSD, but it is also very important to include current problems. Most people with PTSD know that it is impossible to go back and change the reality of the past. Science fiction is one thing, reality is another. However, some focus on the past can help people understand how they filter the present through their memories of the past. Knowing that can help them learn to re-route their thinking.

Again, Bill Mauldin captured an important part of the potential development of PTSD in his cartoon of Willie offering Joe a pair of clean, dry socks as reward for saving his (Willie's) life. On the surface, that may seem like a ridiculous idea. However, anyone who has been in the continuous threat to life and limb can understand the gift of a "clean pair of dry socks." The comparison of life's worth and clean, dry socks can be readily appreciated by those who have "been there."

That's the way support groups can work. Those who have "been there," can and do understand like no others can.

It is my opinion that a support group can be helpful if it focuses on both the cause and the effect (the past, present, and future) of PTSD. If you have PTSD, and you know of a support group, go. Feel free to talk about life, death, and clean dry socks with others that know what you are talking about.

PROFESSIONAL COUNSELING

In the 1960s the United States was going through a cultural revolution. Vietnam veterans were part of the focus of that revolution. Another big issue was the "establishment." The rebels in the revolution were revolting against the established order of the time. That revolution carried over into the field of counseling and psychotherapy. Different methods of doing counseling seemed to "mushroom." Two areas of the establishment in the mental health field involved physical treatment and psychoanalysis. Physical treatment included electroshock therapy, insulin shock therapy and lobotomies. Psychoanalysis was generally Freudian, but Jungian techniques were also prevalent. (Medication was just beginning.) Psychiatrists dominated the scene, but some young revolutionists came up with some strange variations of "therapy." One such example was nude encounter groups. (I personally don't recommend nude encounter groups for the treatment of PTSD.)

Professional counseling can be helpful (and sometimes necessary for the treatment of PTSD), but you may want to have "more than one or two grains of salt" when considering professional counseling. There are still many varieties of help out there. If you are considering going to a professional counselor, don't hesitate to ask questions about the philosophy of counselors you may be considering. I have had training in several different methods of therapy. The techniques that I personally have found to be most helpful include cognitive/behavior methods. Those are types I have discussed in the chapters: Relaxation; Biofeedback; and Instant Replay (cognitive restructuring or "re-routing thought patterns").

As I said, professional counseling can be helpful and even necessary. However, feel free to check out any counselor you consider.

MEDICATION

There is no medication that I know of that will "cure" PTSD. However, I believe that there are some that can ease a little of the pain of PTSD. Being a psychologist, I do not prescribe medication. I also do not give advice about specific medications. My advice to people with PTSD is to talk to their personal physicians about medication. (For people with no personal or primary physician, I advise them to get one.)

One thing I do advise against is self-medication. Alcohol and street chemicals can complicate PTSD. Some Vietnam veterans learned in the war to use readily available chemicals to ease the stress of the trauma of war. In World War II, I was issued two ounces of rye whiskey after each combat mission. This was done by the Army Air Corp. It may have been a temporary help for stress, but it became an addiction for some. Some Vietnam veterans are victims of addiction to chemicals in addition to having PTSD. For those unfortunate souls, I recommend that they get treatment for the addiction as well as treatment for the PTSD. I do this because I believe that treatment for PTSD alone will not be very effective for those with addiction to chemicals.

I use the word chemicals on purpose. Medications are chemicals. They are derived from chemical formulas. If we think of medications as being chemicals, it makes it easier to consider the fact that two different chemicals combined can make a third chemical that may or may not be helpful, or could even be harmful.

A case in point. I have been told that in the Gulf War, the warriors were required to take three different chemicals to help them survive chemical warfare. (There is an irony in this.) After the war, the Pentagon and the Department of Veteran's affairs stated that none of these chemicals were toxic so that they couldn't be contributing to the so-called "Gulf War Syndrome." However, two different universities tested the combination of the required chemicals and found that the combined chemicals made a new chemical that was indeed toxic!

There is an important lesson in this Gulf War problem. That lesson is, do not trust the combinations of self-medication chemicals. Go to a knowledgeable physician for any medication. Be sure and give the physician a list of all chemicals you are using. Then, see that the physician follows up on any side effects you may experience.

Also, be very careful to follow the directions that come from the pharmacy. Develop some method to keep track of the medications. I believe it is best if the person taking the medications assumes responsibility for managing the taking procedure. However, if that is not possible, someone else may have to step in and assume that responsibility.

Another aspect of all of this relates to the need for medication for more than PTSD. It is very important for a prescribing physician to be aware of all chemicals being taken, and to carefully monitor the results. With this in mind, it seems plain to me that self-medication in addition to prescribed medication can be a dangerous thing.

Four areas to consider in relation to PTSD are anxiety; depression; sleep deprivation; and rage. These are very often an important part of PTSD, but they are sometimes lost in the shuffle of PTSD. It may be that these four parts may need to be diagnosed in addition to PTSD so that they are not lost in the shuffle. There are prescription medications that can help these parts. Easing some of the pain of any or all of these can make it possible to use counseling more effectively. It is also important to remember that new medications come along. Keep in touch with any physician who prescribes medications for you.

RELIGION AND PRAYER

Religion and prayer can be helpful for some people with PTSD. However, there can be some problems with this approach. Many people with PTSD have a difficult time with churches, organizations, or any kind of crowds. For some people it is possible to combine prayer with the relaxation and breathing exercises that have been described in previous chapters.

I became interested in prayer and stress management methods soon after I became certified in biofeedback. At that time I had a woman referred to me for biofeedback because she hyperventilated. She would go into panic attacks and start breathing so fast and in so shallow a manner that she would sometimes pass out. Her husband came with her to my office because she was afraid to drive. He came in to the consultation office with her. I hooked her up with the biofeedback instruments and started her on the relaxation procedures. At that point, the husband jumped up and said, "Stop! You are teaching my wife to meditate!"

I, of course, stopped the procedure and asked the man to tell me what the problem was. He then explained that meditation was heathen, and against their religion. He said that meditation came from India and that made it heathen. Nothing I could say at that time could convince the man that biofeedback was developed in the U. S. of A. Therefore, I resolved to research the subject.

After careful research, I wrote the book *Prayer Power and Stress Management* (Bedford, 1983). That book describes how early Christians combined prayers and breathing in a way that startled me by the similarities of it with modern day biofeedback. These Christians became known as the "Desert Fathers." These people (both men and women) lived very simple lives in the desert areas in the fourth century. Since both men and women used these methods, I chose to call them "Desert Christians."

With my research, I also learned that ancient Jews also had meditative and breathing techniques. The Jewish methods were part of what they called Kabbalah. And some of those methods went back before Moses. All this proved to my satisfaction that meditation was no more heathen than was breathing,.The Desert Christians believed that if they combined a short prayer with their breathing, they would eventually be saying a prayer every time they took a breath. Paul's message "to pray without ceasing" (Thessalonians I 5:17), had a deep influence on them. They believed that they could combine short prayers with breathing and that that way, they would be praying night and day—even in their sleep.

Few people today could live the simple lives the Desert Christians lived in the fourth century. Some Vietnam veterans today would like to live simple lives in the solitude of wilderness areas. Most of those veterans would be glad to trade most anything for the intrusive thoughts of war. I'm not suggesting that these veterans can get rid of their intrusive thoughts by "praying without ceasing." I am suggesting that anyone can get some relief from the chemicals of stress by getting in the habit of doing a Q R (quieting response) every twenty minutes, or anytime they feel stress building. I am also suggesting that saying a short prayer (or phrase) can add to the benefit of breathing—and remember, I don't think that breathing is heathen.

One of my favorite short prayers (or phrases) is, "Peace be with us." With that one, you think, "Peace," as you take a deep breath in through your nose. Then, relax your face, neck, and shoulders as you exhale and think, "be with us." This won't cure PTSD or intrusive thoughts, but it won't hurt.

I wish that I had known about all this when I was sitting in the tail turret of a B-24 in World War II. It might have helped some with the intrusive thoughts I always had. I do remember saying a prayer on one occasion. When I started having nightmares about being called back into service at the start of The Gulf War, I wrote it as part of my book, *The Wild Blue Yonder* (Bedford, 1992).

This is how that prayer went: "Tail gunner to God; Come in God. We have a ME109 at twelve o'clock high, and closing fast. God help me kill this Nazi Fiend, he's trying to kill me. What's that God, over? You say he's praying the same prayer. But God, he's the enemy. What's that God, over? You say if I have enemies, I too am an enemy. There, he just flew under. We both missed. What's that, God, over? You say, better luck next time to both of us! Say, who are you anyway, over. You say you're Thor, the God of War, over and out."

That "prayer" didn't help. I remember one that did. When we were roaring down the runway on take off for a mission, those of us in the back of the plane sat on the floor with our backs to the bomb bay bulkhead. The roar of the four big engines and the vibrations in my chest always reminded me of my younger years in church. The church my dear mother took us to had a huge organ. My mother insisted that we sit near the front of the church. When we sang the Doxology, the organ boomed especially loud. I used to like the vibrations in my chest during that singing and booming.

With those pleasant thoughts in mind during the chest vibrations on take off, I always sang the Doxology. "Praise God from whom all blessings flow. Praise Him, all creatures here below. Praise Him above, ye heavenly host, praise Father, Son, and Holy Ghost."

That singing helped me some with the stress of take off. It didn't do a lot for my crewmates. They thought I was losing my mind. However, my crewmates were so busy trying not to lose their minds that they didn't say much to me.

I also had conversations with God when I crawled into the bomb bay to arm the bombs. I was the armorer gunner as well as the tail gunner and I had to crawl along a ten-inch runway without a parachute (there wasn't room between the bomb bay struts for a chute). I had special conversations with God when I had to do the arming of the bombs with the bomb bay doors open (and the ground about two miles down). I don't think those conversations helped any more than the "calling God" one above.

Enough of my current intrusive thoughts. Back to the short prayers and Q R's (quieting response). Using that technique doesn't have to change any prayer methods you may already be using. You also don't have to use one with every breath, as did the Desert Christians. However, the method can help with stress management.

Leaving religion aside, here's how the method works from a

physiological standpoint. When we start to get stressed, we breathe a little faster in a little more shallow manner. When we do that, we get a building up of oxygen in our lungs (unless we are running from a saber tooth tiger). When we deliberately take a deep breath and relax, we help keep the balance between oxygen and carbon dioxide in our lungs. That way, our brains read the balance as an "all clear" signal, and tell our adrenal glands to slow down the flow of tiger juice. This all happens whether we include a prayer or not, but I think the use of a short prayer or a peaceful phrase can add a little more to stress management.

As I said, I wish I had known this during World War II. The methods would have been more helpful than the prayers I said then. However, I have found out that we are seldom too old to learn new tricks.

Here is the stress management and prayer method I use now (to help with what PTSD I have).

Every twenty to thirty minutes I try to remember to do a quieting response (Q R). As I take a deep breath in through my nose, I think, "Peace." Then, a few seconds later, I try and relax my upper body and torso as I let the air out slowly and think, "Be with us." That helps focus my concentration on a peaceful feeling, and it keeps a balance in my lungs between oxygen and carbon dioxide. That way, my alligator brain sends a message to my adrenal glands saying, "All clear. Save the tiger juice."

Here is a longer exercise. I get up early in the morning and have a bite to eat. Then, I do what exercise I can, and get my pulse rate up. After that, I lie down and do a relaxation and biofeedback procedure as I do some deep breathing, and take my blood pressure. (Later, I take my blood pressure again to see how fast I can bring it down.) After I have brought my hand temperature up, I say a prayer I wrote for my book, *Prayer Power*. Here is that prayer:

Almighty God, please listen to our prayers and help us quiet our bodies so that our spirits can sense Your wisdom.

Help us love one another and always remember that You are love.

Help us teach others the true meaning of love so that they too can feel Your peace.

Help us accept ourselves and the realities of our lives so that we may do the things we need to do.

Help us remember that Your power is within ourselves and guide us so that we may use this energy with love

We give humble thanks for all You have done for us and we ask You to be with us always so that we can stay united for all eternity in love, and peace, and deep communion.

Hallelujah, Hallelujah, Hallelujah,
Forever and ever,
Amen.

I thought of things important to me when I wrote this prayer, and I chose my short prayer, "Peace—Be with us." If you use this method, you can do some instant replays along with the total method. You can make up your own prayer. Use this one or any that you know. You don't need to change your current prayers, but you could add some new elements that might make PTSD a little less painful.

KILLING AND PTSD

David A. Grossman did an extremely important study on the psychological effects of killing human beings in war. He wrote the book, *On Killing: The Psychological Cost of Learning to Kill in War and Society*, published by Little, Brown and Company (1996). That book is very important reading for anyone trying to understand PTSD. Grossman did an extensive review of the literature and compared the effects of killing in different wars and different war situations. He developed a scale to compare resistance to killing to the physical distance from the target. He concluded that, generally speaking, the closer the killer is to the target, the more resistance there is to killing. However, he pointed out that the closer one is to an enemy, two types of danger exist. One, of course, is the danger of being killed. The other is the psychological cost and danger of seeing the enemy up close and personal in the process of dying.

Grossman discussed the hand-to-hand fighting that went on at close range in the Vietnam War. Then, he discussed the long-range killing that resulted from the air war in World War II. He described in detail the fire bombing of Hamburg, Germany, and he wrote the following:

> Seventy thousand people died at Hamburg the night the air caught fire. They were mostly women, children and the elderly, since those of soldiering age were generally at the front. They died horrible deaths, burning and suffocating. If bomber crewmembers had had to turn a flamethrower on each of these seventy thousand women and children, or worse yet slit each of their throats, the awfulness and trauma inherent in the act would have been of such magnitude that it simply would not have happened. But when it is done from

> thousands of feet in the air, where the screams cannot be heard and the burning bodies cannot be seen, it is easy. (100)

I would agree with Grossman. Bomber crewmembers would have had a very difficult time doing that killing at close range. I was part of a bomber crew in World War II. I was the armorer on the crew so that it was my duty to arm the bombs we dropped. I was also the tail gunner, so that I saw where the bombs hit. Our bombs did not always hit "military" targets. It has been more than 50 years since I helped in the bombing of southern Europe. I still have nightmares about the women, children and elderly people we killed.

As an aircrew, we too talked about targets instead of people. That is a common thing in wars. We dehumanize the enemy to help ease the psychological pain of killing. In Vietnam the enemy became "gooks." In Korea some warriors called the enemy "slants" (for slant eyes). In World War II we also talked about "Nazis" (as well as targets). In World War I, the enemy were "Krauts."

I believe that killing in war can be costly from a psychological standpoint. I believe that there is a connection between the psychological cost of killing and PTSD. I had real fear about enemy fighter planes and the flak of anti-aircraft shells. I have recovered from those fears, but I have not recovered from the revulsion of seeing bombs that I armed miss targets and kill civilian people.

Many people in America have been upset about the massacre of Mylai, and the media described in detail the killing of a hundred Vietnamese. How many of those people remember the fire bombing of Hamburg? People have been upset by the Nazi death chambers, but how have those same people felt about the mass killing of people in Dresden where 80 thousand died cruel and painful deaths? Grossman wrote the following:

> ...Throughout World War II bomber crews on both sides killed millions of women, children, and elderly people, no different from their own wives, children, and parents. The pilots, navigators, bombardiers, and gunners in these aircraft were able to bring themselves

> to kill these civilians primarily through application of the mental leverage provided to them by the distance factor.
>
> Intellectually, they understood the horror of what they were doing. Emotionally, the distance involved permitted them to deny it. (102)

I will say again, some of us had trouble "denying" it. Some of us have developed some PTSD as a result of, "the psychological cost of learning to kill in war." I believe that the horror of killing plays as important a role in the development of PTSD as the fear of being killed.

I believe that the stress system was given to us to help us survive in a world of danger from attack by carnivorous predators wanting to eat us. Our ancestors needed extra strength to fight the hungry creatures, or to run from them if possible. I don't know what they called these systems. We now call the systems our fight-or-flight reactions. As noted before, these systems can provide human beings with extra energy when we are being attacked.

Our ancient ancestors also ate meat so that they too were predators. They had to kill other creatures to get that meat. And, in a world of jungle principles, the system of war probably emerged. Since killing seems to be a part of war, our ancient ancestors started killing each other, probably to gain more territory to hunt game. We don't have written records of this early combat, but we do have artifacts. These ancient fighters used rocks, clubs and spears. It may have been that the first efforts to develop killing at a distance involved arrows and catapults. Then, when they learned to forge metal, swords and knives probably came into use. I have heard that gunpowder was developed by the Chinese and was first used in fireworks. Europe became aware of gunpowder over 700 years ago, and the European military saw potentials for cannons and guns. With gunpowder, warfare changed. The element of "distance" came into being with the cannons and rifles.

When war was mainly hand-to-hand fighting, the fight-or-flight part of the stress system was probably helpful. Warriors needed a lot of extra energy to do their killing. When it became possible to kill from a distance, the fight-or-flight system became less important from a positive standpoint. This has become more and more of a reality when distance and remote control are involved in weapons and war. In the mid-1980s it was possible for one aircraft to carry more explosive power than all of the explosive power used in all wars up until that time. Now we have missiles that can be fired from thousands of miles. That way, millions of people can be killed by remote control. The thought of that is enough to activate my PTSD. I don't know how a human being could trigger such a device without developing PTSD—if they were hooked up to the reality of what they were doing.

In the Vietnam War, close contact with the enemy and distance and remoteness were involved in killing. I believe that those factors, plus the emphasis on "body count" played a part in the number of Vietnam veterans that have developed PTSD.

VIOLATION OF WHAT'S RIGHT

Most veterans with PTSD that I have counseled have had negative reactions to the violation of what they think is right. And, many of those veterans seem to me to be trapped in their own anger and rage. They have experienced, "intense fear, helplessness, and horror." These feelings have been related to firefights, ambushes, and seeing death and destruction all around them. These feelings represent the first criteria for the diagnosis of PTSD in the *American Psychiatric Association Diagnostic and Statistic Manual of the American Psychiatric Association*. (And the VA uses the *DSM* as their "Bible.") However, I have listened to many deeper memories of "the violation of what's right."

Many veterans of the Vietnam War believe that that war itself was a violation of what's right. I believe that these feelings play a part in the fact that PTSD is such a stubborn disorder, I think it is sad that the DSM does not recognize the violation of what's right as criteria for establishing PTSD as a disorder. I also believe that it is even sadder that the VA (Veteran's Association) goes along with the DSM.

A psychiatrist, Jonathon Shay, M.D., Ph.D. has written a very scholarly and fascinating book, *Achilles in Vietnam, Combat Trauma and the Undoing of Character* (Shay, 1994). In his book, Dr. Shay described an in-depth study comparing Homer's work, *The Iliad*, and the Vietnam War. He described the similarity of the experiences Achilles and Vietnam warriors. The book has a main theme of the violation of what's right which Dr. Shay calls, "themis." Dr. Shay states that he believes that the violation of themis (what's right) can and does lead to inner rage that he feels is a life long thing.

Dr. Shay states:

> ...I've come to strongly believe through my work

> with Vietnam veterans that moral injury is an essential part of any combat trauma that leads to lifelong psychological injury. Veterans can usually recover from horror, fear and grief once they return to civilian life so long as "what's right" has not been violated. (20)

I whole-heartedly agree with Dr. Shay. In more than fifty years since World War II, I have recovered from fear of enemy antiaircraft artillery (flak) and my duels with Nazi pilots in Messerschmit fighter planes. I have not recovered from my revulsions of seeing bombs that I personally armed, landing in civilian areas. That is my violation of what was right. My "themis" related to our bombardier who tried to handle his trauma of war with bourbon. I did not personally see the bombardier drunk in the front of our bomber on the flight deck under extra flak jackets. I knew first hand that he never came near the bombs when I armed them (a part of his job). I was told by the nose gunner that he (the nose gunner) was ordered to toggle our bombs over targets. I personally heard the nose gunner call out, "Bombs Away." The other two enlisted men in the front of the plane told me about the bombardier's bourbon. I personally saw our bombs landing in civilian areas that the higher command called "collateral damage."

No, I have not recovered from my conception of the violation of what's right. Added insult to my psychic injury came when I had to lie about our crew's snafus. I have tried to go beyond all this, but I have not been successful in that endeavor. I have concluded that if I haven't recovered in more than 50 years, that the PTSD that I have has made my psychic injury very stubborn if not permanent. It now seems ironic to me that the VA does not want to recognize this injury, or even talk about it. I don't know if I ever hit a Nazi pilot, but I have vivid memories (and nightmares) of bombs I armed killing women, children and old people. I have not found any chemical or therapeutic techniques to wipe out those memories. I also did not find it very consoling when a VA psychologist told me, "Next time, don't look!" I do hope and pray that there will never be a "next time" for me or any other human being.

SUMMARY AND CONCLUSIONS

The official history of Post-Traumatic Stress Disorder (PTSD) goes back to 1980 when the diagnosis was first introduced into the American Psychiatric Association Diagnostic and Statistical Manual.

The history of war goes back before written records were kept. I believe that the real history of PTSD goes back long before 1980. The human stress reaction probably goes back in history to ancient times. Maybe it goes back as far as the history of war. I would propose that the history of PTSD might go back to the time in history when the human stress reaction was no longer helpful in war.

When ancient wars were fought with stones, clubs, knives, and swords, the warriors probably fought more efficiently with the added energy coming from the fight-or-flight part of their stress reactions. Then, when distance began to become a factor in war with the development of weapons such as bows and arrows, spears, catapults, guns, and cannons, extra energy of the fight-of-flight reaction began to be less important. However, I am sure that the general stress of war kept warriors' fight-or-flight reactions going strong. That way, the human stress reaction could have started to be part of the problem of war rather than a help. The factor of distance in war meant that warriors directed artificial energy (cannons, airplanes and missiles) to deliver destruction to the enemy. Now, human beings have the technology to deliver incredible amounts of destruction with no more energy than it takes to push a few buttons. With the factor of distance and remote energy, the element of time enters in. The human beings that push the buttons may not be "connected" directly to awareness of the destruction they are delivering to human beings. The element of time is involved in the "post" part of Post-Traumatic Stress Disorder. People who "look back" on what they have done in destroying other people could begin to recognize their own part in the trauma of war. That way they can develop stress long after they participated in the original trauma.

I realize that these ideas represent an over simplification of the very complex problem of PTSD. However, I do believe that the ideas can be a part of PTSD. And, as human beings develop more technical (and devious) methods of delivering powerful instruments of destruction, with distance and remote control as factors, we would be well advised to make sure that the button pushers are fully aware of all of the costs of war, including the emotional costs.

As has been stated many times, I don't know a sure-fire method of curing PTSD. I do have some ideas of how to prevent PTSD from war. That would be to prevent wars.

I wish I had the answer to why human beings have fought so many wars. I wish I had the wisdom to pass on to future generations to prevent others from going to war. In the years since World War II, I have studied human psychology in depth, but I haven't found the answer. I have come to believe that we as human beings must find the answer if this world and human beings are to survive. I have some thoughts, but they are only pieces—my pieces—to the global concept we must formulate to go beyond war.

First of all, we need to recognize the potentials of the human brain. So far, few of us have tapped into the full capacity of the human brain. We must remember that human brains have the capacity to save the world, and they have the capacity to destroy the world. I believe we are at a point in time when we have to have a mass decision regarding that choice.

I believe that a piece of the puzzle relates to the fact that we have marvelous brains, but we live in biological bodies that are geared to survival by physical force. Unfortunately, our brains have allowed us to develop physical force that goes beyond all reason. We now have instruments of destruction that allow one airplane to carry more explosive power than that that has been used in all previous wars—and that in one bomb run! I was part of a combat aircrew in World War II. That was a primitive war compared to the type of war that is possible as we enter the 21st century.

Another piece of the puzzle is related to emotions and the fight-or-flight part of the human stress reaction. We have been provided with this fight-or-flight system to help us survive saber tooth tigers.

It would take a lot of energy to run from a saber tooth tiger or fight to save ourselves if we couldn't run. In addition to these primitive systems, we have complex brains that include the reptilian complex (I call these parts our alligator brains); the mammalian layers; and our cortexes. The answer to going beyond war will need to come from our cerebral cortexes as our alligator brains only know how to activate running and/or fighting.

When we look back on the history of war, most wars have been started by ideas. We find that one faction is usually the aggressor, and the other faction is usually defending itself. But, when we look at the "last straws" that have triggered attacks, they have usually related to power struggles; territorial disputes; cultural differences; and other nutty ideas.

When modern wars are started, we don't use our fight-or-flight systems as nature intended. We use intricate technology that allows us to fight by remote control. As I look back on my war experiences (through the lenses of my psychological knowledge), I have to admit that I was activating a great deal of stress energy in the fight, but that the energy activated became a problem itself. It really didn't take tremendous energy to operate the hydraulic system in my tail turret that allowed me to aim and fire two fifty-caliber machine guns. I don't recall much anger at the time I fired my guns. I recall a great deal of fear. My body was preparing me to run, but my brain was directing me to fight with the remote control apparatus available to me.

One of the ideas I am struggling with here relates to the idea that we as human beings are primitive creatures who have tremendous brain power to develop instruments of war that are unbelievably powerful. When we turn our alligator brains loose with these instruments, we can easily destroy the world in which we live. I believe that if we can accept our primitive natures, we can learn to better manage the instincts we have to fight saber tooth tigers or to run from them. I, therefore, believe that a missing part of our puzzle is education. I firmly believe that we must put emphasis on educating human beings rather than emphasis on developing more diabolic instruments to destroy human beings.

Another idea whose time is coming has to do with sex. I think that more wars have been started by males than by females. I believe that females have the capacity to fight, and if you doubt this, think of the mother bear protecting her cubs. However, I don't think that there are many females who are ready to fight just to prove that they are females. On the other hand, there are many males who will fight to the death just to prove that they are males! And, unfortunately, many such males struggle into leadership roles that allow them to decide to go to war for this proof. Some of these leaders sit near the red buttons that could destroy our world. (Some even carry remote buttons around in attaché cases when they get away from the buttons on their desks.)

In today's world we cannot allow our alligator brains to unleash our fight-or-flight systems made up of nuclear powered explosives. We cannot afford to be willing to destroy our world in disputes that involve a few miles of territory. We cannot afford to unleash this power to demonstrate our masculinity.

Another concept I have come to consider since the war relates to an apparent need for enemies by some people. I believe that some political candidates have taken advantage of this need. In some instances, this type of manipulation can lead to the promotion of a war stance. And when we maintain a war stance, declaration of war can be close at hand. Thoughts along this line remind me of President Dwight Eisenhower's comment about our country's need to beware of our military-industrial complex. I think his warning was pertinent then and is pertinent now.

I am in hopes that the "one hundred monkey" theory may some day be put into play in regard to the end of war. In this, there might be enough people who will spontaneously reach a conclusion that our world must go beyond war. This theory is said to describe the behavior of some monkeys living on islands in the Far East near Japan. The story goes that these monkeys were fed by people dumping sweet potatoes on the beaches of the islands. Then one day, one little girl monkey started washing her sweet potatoes in the sea before eating them in order to wash off the sand. At first the other monkeys ignored her, but gradually other monkeys on her island began to follow her example. The story goes on to the effect that when one hundred monkeys on the island started washing their sweet potatoes, the monkeys on the other islands started washing their sweet potatoes even though they had never seen the monkeys on the little girl monkey's island wash theirs.

I believe the Bible says something about hammering swords into plowshares and there is a spiritual song, "I ain't going to study war no more." Both of these ideas are close to my heart. I believe that in addition to hammering our swords into plows, we need to invest much more energy and resources into realistic education of the world's children. If monkeys can, why can't we?

Since starting the project of reviewing my war experiences, I have been speculating about how human beings can try to be as smart as the monkeys. I believe we must review some of the findings of the Nuremberg trials held after World War II. These were trials of people labeled as "war criminals." These people represented some of the leaders of the Nazi movement. An important thing to consider here was the frequent defense put forward by many of these people. That defense was, "I was following orders." This seems to be a form of "buck passing."

An idea that is dear to my heart relates to educating our young people and passing some of the buck back to them in our voting process. An informed vote is a priceless thing. I would fight for that again, but I would hope that I would not have to kill innocent civilians in the process. I have not gotten over that part of the war.

I believe that the development of PTSD in relation to war is a complicated process. I think that the killing of human beings plays as important a part in PTSD as the fear of being killed. I also believe that service personnel who assist war efforts have potential for the development of PTSD. That goes beyond the criteria in the *Diagnostic and Statistical Manual (DSM) of the American Psychiatric Association*. The belief comes from counseling war veterans who were not "out in the bush," but were assisting war efforts. This is particularly true when war efforts involve killing civilians as well as enemy combat troops. This is becoming more and more important as we develop instruments of mass destruction.

One purpose for writing this book was to help people with PTSD learn to cope with the disorder. Another purpose was to help people who live with others who have PTSD. They too can live happier lives if they learn more about the disorder and develop more coping skills.

Another important purpose was to point out the emotional cost of war. I believe that the people responsible for planning wars would be well advised to include as they plan for war the emotional costs in the cost of weapons and the logistics of war.

I would like to believe that human beings will eventually think in terms of going beyond war, I realize that until such time, we have to keep enough armed forces to defend our country. I also realize that until such time as human beings go beyond war, PTSD will be a spin-off of war. Therefore, it is important for us to understand Post-Traumatic Stress Disorder. PTSD is not restricted to war, but war certainly can contribute to PTSD. And, PTSD goes far beyond the horror of dying in combat.

BIBLIOGRAPHY

Ambrose, Stephen E. (1997): *Citizen Soldiers*. New York, NY: Simon and Schuster.

American Psychiatric Association: *Diagnostic and Statistical Manual of Mental Disorders, Fourth Edition*. Washington, DC, American Psychiatric Association, 1994.

Bach, George, and Wyden, Peter (1968): *The Intimate Enemy: How to fight fair in love and marriage*. New York, NY: Avon Books.

Baker, Mark (1983): *NAM: The Vietnam War in the Words of the Men and Women Who Fought There*. New York, NY: Berkley Books.

Beck, Aaron; Rush, John; Shaw, Brian; Emery, Gary (1979): *Cognitive Therapy of Depression*. New York, NY: The Guilford Press.

Bedford, Stewart (1974): *Instant Replay*. New York, NY: The Institute for Rational Living, Inc.

Bedford, Stewart (1980): *Stress and Tiger Juice: How to manage your stress and improve your life and health*. Chico, CA: Scott Publications.

Bedford, Stewart (1981): *Tiger Juice: A Book About Stress for Kids (of all ages)*. Chico, CA: Scott Publications.

Bedford, Stewart, Foreward by Selye, Hans (1983): *Prayer Power and Stress Management*. Chico, CA: A & S Press.

Bedford, Stewart (1992): *The Wild Blue Yonder*. Chico, CA: Chico Psych Center.

Benson, Herbert with Klipper, Miriam (1975): *The Relaxation Response*. New York, NY: William Morrow and Company.

Berman, Larry (1982): *Planning a Tragedy: The Americanization of The War in Vietnam*. New York, NY: Norton, 1982.

Cain, Jonathan (1984): *Saigon Commandos: Boonie-Rat Body Burning #5*. New York, NY: Zebra Books.

Cannon, Walter (1932): *The Wisdom of the Body*. New York, NY: W.W. Norton.

Ehrenreich, Barbara (1997): *Blood Rites: Origins and History of the Passions of War*. New York, NY: Metropolitan Books, Henry

Holt and Company, Inc.

Ellis, Albert and Tafrate, Raymond (1997): *How to Control Your Anger Before It Controls You.* Toronto, Canada: Carol Publishing Group.

Faas, Horst and Page, Tim, Editors (1997): *Requiem: By the Photographers Who Died in Vietnam and Indochina.* New York, NY: Random House.

Foy, David W., Editor (1992): *Treating PTSD: Cognitive-Behavioral Strategies.* New York, NY: The Guilford Press.

Goldberger, Leo, and Breznitz, Editors (1982): *Handbook of Stress: Theoretical and Clinical Aspects.* New York, NY: The Free Press.

Gordon, Thomas (1964): *Parent Effectiveness Training.* Pasadena, CA: Gordon.

Grinker, R.R. and Spiegel, J.J. (1945): *Men Under Stress.* Philadelphia, PA: Blakiston.

Grossman, Dave (1996): *On Killing: The Psychological Cost of Learning to Kill in War and Society.* New York, NY: Back Bay Books.

Hanson, Peter G. (1986): *The Joy of Stress.* New York, NY: Andrews, McMeel and Parker.

Heller, Joseph (1961): *Catch-22.* New York, NY: A Dell Book.

Jacobson, Edmund (1962): *You Must Relax.* New York, NY: McGraw-Hill Book Company.

Kahin, George M.; Lewis, John W. (1969): *The United States in Vietnam.* New York, NY: Dell Publishing Co. Inc.

Karow, Stanley (1997): *Vietnam: A History.* USA: Penguin Books.

Kovic, Ron (1976): *Born on the Fourth of July.* New York, NY: Pocket Books.

Kubey, Craig; Addleston, David; O'Dell, Richard; Snyder, Keith; Stichman, Barton; and Vietnam Veterans of America (1985): *The Vietnam Vet Survival Guide: How to Cut Through the Bureaucacy and Get What You Need and Are Entitled To.* New York, NY: Ballantine Books.

Lamott, Kenneth (1975): *Escape From Stress: Learning Relaxation With the Right Response.* New York, NY: Berkley Publishing Corporation.

Leninger, Jack (1993): *Time Heals No Wounds*. New York, NY: Ivy Books.

Lifton, Robert Jay (1973): *Home From the War: Vietnam Veterans Neither Victims nor Executioners*. New York, NY: Simon and Schuster.

Lorenz, Konrad (1966). *On Aggression*. New York, NY: Harcourt, Brace and World, Inc.

Mason, Patience H. C. (1990): *Recovering From the War: A Woman's Guide to Helping Your Vietnam Vet, Your Family, and Yourself.* New York, NY: Viking Penguin.

Mason, Robert (1983): *Chickenhawk*. New York, NY: The Viking Press.

Maudlin, Bill (1944): *Up Front*. New York, NY: Henry Holt and Company.

Maultsby, Maxie C. Jr., and Hendricks, Allie (1974): *You and Your Emotions*. Lexington, Kentucky: University Medical Center.

McKay, Mathew; Rogers, Peter; McKay, Judith (1989): *When Anger Hurts: Quieting the Storm Within*. Oakland, CA: New Harbinger Publications.

McMaster, H.R. (1997): *Dereliction of Duty: Lyndon Johnson, Robert McNamara, The Joint Chiefs of Staff, and the Lies That Led to Vietnam*. New York, NY: Harper Collins Publishers.

Meichenbaum, Donald (1994): *A Clinical Handbook/Practical Therapist Manual for Assessing and Treating Adults with Post-Traumatic Stress Disorder (PTSD)*. Waterloo, Ontario, Canada; Institute Press.

Merrick, Monte (1990): *Memphis Belle*. New York, NY: Berkley Books.

Orenstein, Robert and Sobel, David (1987): *The Healing Brain Breakthrough Discoveries About How the Brain Keeps Us Healthy*. New York, NY: Simon and Schuster.

Page, Tim and Pimlott, John, Editors (1988): *Nam: The Vietnam Experience 1965-1975*. London: Orbis Publishing Ltd.

Pelletier, Kenneth (1977): *Mind as Healer: Mind as Slayer*. New York, NY: A Delta Book.

Pimlott, John (1988): *NAM: The Vietnam Experience: 1965-1975*. London: Octopus Publishing Group Ltd.

Plaster, John L. (1997): *SOG: The Secret Wars of America's Commandos in Vietnam*. New York, NY: Simon and Shuster.

Safer, Morley (1990): *Flashbacks on Returning to Vietnam*. New York, NY: Random House.

Santoli, Al (1985): *To Bear Any Burden: The Vietname War and Its Aftermath in the Words of Americans and Southeast Asians*. New York, NY, NY: Ballantine Books.

Sapolsky, Robert M. (1996): *Science*; Vol. 273, 9 August.

Sapolsky, Robert M. (1998): *Why Zebras Don't Get Ulcers*. New York, NY: W.H. Freeman and Company.

Schafer, Walt (1983): *Wellness Through Stress Management*. Davis, CA: International Dialogue Press.

Selye, Hans (1976): *The Stress of Life*. New York, NY: McGraw-Hill Book Company.

Shay, Jonathan, M.D., PH.D. (1994): *Achilles in Vietnam: Comat Trauma and the Undoing of Character*. New York: Simon & Schuster.

Sheehan, Neil (1988): *A Bright Shining Lie: John Paul Vann and America in Vietnam*. New York, NY: Vintage Books.

Stinson, Joseph; Carabatos, James (1986): *Heartbreak Ridge*. New York, NY: Warner Books.

Stroebel, Charles F. (1976): *Quieting Response Training*. New York, NY: Biomonitoring Applications.

Trumbo, Dalton (1939): *Johnny Got His Gun*. New York, NY: J. B. Lippincott.

Vanderkolk, Bessel; McFarlane, Alexander; Weisaeth, Lars; Editors (1996): *Traumatic Stress: The Effects of Overwhelming Experience on Mind, Body, and Society*. New York, NY: The Guilford Press.

VanDevanter, Lynda with Morgan, Christopher (1983): *Home Before Morning: The True Story of an Army Nurse in Vietnam*. New York, NY: Warner Books.

Williams, Tom, Editor (1987): *Post-Traumatic Stress Disorder: A Book for Clinicians*. Cincinnati, OH: Disabled American Veterans.

Printed in the United States
24887LVS00001B/256-258